Engaging Beneficiaries for Development Participation

Engaging Beneficiaries for Development Participation:

When, How, and To What Extent?

By

Nandita Dutta

Cambridge Scholars Publishing

Engaging Beneficiaries for Development Participation:
When, How, and To What Extent?

By Nandita Dutta

This book first published 2023

Cambridge Scholars Publishing

Lady Stephenson Library, Newcastle upon Tyne, NE6 2PA, UK

British Library Cataloguing in Publication Data
A catalogue record for this book is available from the British Library

ISBN (10): 1-5275-1267-3
ISBN (13): 978-1-5275-1267-2

To my parents Chitta Ranjan Datta & Bani Datta
– my mentors, my inspirations

TABLE OF CONTENTS

List of Figures, Tables and Boxes

Figures

Tables

Boxes

FOREWORD

Now, more than ever, community participation and engagement in community development is essential. With the United Nations' call for reduced inequalities, sustainable cities and communities, industry, innovation and infrastructure, decent work and economic growth, no poverty, good health and wellbeing, and many other key goals (United Nations, 2015), prioritising beneficiary engagement is essential, particularly in developing nations. This book presents a topic that is seldom discussed in the development field – how development participation is achieved in the Bangladesh context. It presents the idea that how and when beneficiaries are engaged influences the extent of, and outcomes of, participation. It's a novel concept, and the book, Engaging Beneficiaries for Development Participation: When, How and to What Extent? is thoroughly researched to present comprehensive recommendations.

Nandita Dutta has explored development participation in Bangladesh, a country which hosts many NGOs that work together to undertake the country's development agenda. An explanation of terminologies is provided and the planning and implementation of development interventions by integrating people in the process is explored in detail, as ideas for beneficiary engagement are proposed.

This book offers insightful references to the country's development planning and strategies which are specifically related to people-oriented development, starting from the first five-year plan in 1973. A framework of how people-oriented concepts gradually progressed and integrated into the country's development planning is also incorporated.

NGOs connect with beneficiaries to give them access to development. Whether the public sector can engage beneficiaries has seldom been discussed in the development literature. This book reveals how some of the government departments are responsible for engaging beneficiaries in the pursuit of development participation. NGOs find it helpful to partner with the government to carry out their development agenda. Rather than achieving participation alone, NGOs prefer to work closely with the government, private sector and UPs to help these organisations to reach beneficiaries at the grassroots level.

One issue raised in this book is that NGOs are not the only institution to connect beneficiaries, and in fact, NGOs work in competition, or perhaps, with, Governments to engage beneficiaries. While arguing that beneficiary engagement is a prerequisite for development participation, this book reveals that it takes place within government and NGO project settings associated with many other enabling factors. The book also raises a few concerns, such as the future of participation in the absence of projects, and whether participation in development is still a priority.

This well researched book contributes an understanding of development from the perspective of the institutions responsible, and also the beneficiaries at the grassroot levels. Within a contemporary understanding of developing countries, and engaging with community participation, this book fills an important gap in the market. I commend Dutta for her work on this. Within the chaotic and rapidly changing global environment, a greater understanding of development, and community participation is needed. This book can enable the beginning of many conversations around this space, and development plans to be implemented.

Professor Raechel Johns, Canberra Business School,
University of Canberra

ACKNOWLEDGEMENTS

I acknowledge the Ngunnawal people as the traditional custodians of the land upon which I have been living, studying and writing this book. I also pay my respects to First Nations Elders past and present.

I completed my PhD at the Faculty of Arts and Design, University of Canberra, Australia. I would never have been able to continue my studies without the support I received from the university. This book is adapted from my PhD thesis "Engaging Project Beneficiaries: A Comparative Analysis of Government and NGO Practises in the Development Context of Bangladesh." I would like to thank the supervisory panel, associate professors Dr Tahmina Rashid and Dr Bethaney Turner, for guiding me to the completion of the degree.

I started my career in the Bangladesh civil service in 1995. I strongly believe that this was the foundation for what I have achieved today. I pay my respect to the people of Bangladesh, who are striving hard to sustain their achievements in various areas that ultimately contributes to upscaling the country's socio-economic conditions. The information on development planning and policies on the Government of Bangladesh website contributed enormously to my PhD, and helped me to crosscheck information and establish my arguments. I must acknowledge this initiative of the Government of Bangladesh.

I would like to thank the research participants who gave me their time despite their busy schedules. I must also acknowledge the help I received from my friends and colleagues in the Bangladesh civil service, UNDP and officials in NGOs in conducting the fieldwork that contributed to the discussions in this book. I am grateful for having wonderful colleagues at the faculty of Business, Government and Law here at the University of Canberra, who always encouraged me to continue in my academic adventures and appreciated my achievements.

I am thankful to my parents, who spent their lives for one single purpose – the education for their daughters. Finally, I owe much to my sister Shilpy Dutta, my husband Biraj Khajanchi, our son Himalaya Khajanchi and my in-laws for their unconditional support and encouragement on this publication. I am grateful for having a supportive family, which is essential for a woman to move forward.

Nandita Dutta

LIST OF ABBREVIATIONS

ADB	Asian Development Bank
ADP	Annual Development Programme
ASA	Association of Social Advancement
BARD	Bangladesh Academy for Rural Development
BBS	Bangladesh Bureau of Statistics
BDT	Currency of Bangladesh
BPATC	Bangladesh Public Administration Training Centre
BRAC	Bangladesh Rural Advancement Committee
BTRC	Bangladesh Telecommunications Regulatory Commission
CDRF	Capacity Development Results Framework
CHT	Chittagong Hill Tracts
DAE	Department of Agriculture Extension
DMB	Disaster Management Bureau
DPP	Development Project Proforma
DWA	Directorate of Women Affairs
ERD	Economic Relations Division
ESDO	Eco Social Development Organisation
FDI	Foreign Development Index
FGD	Focus-group discussion
FWV	Family-welfare volunteer
FY	Financial year
FYPs	Five Year Plan
GED	General Economic Division
GOs	Government Organisations
GOB	Government of Bangladesh
GSS	Gono Shahajjo Sangstha
HDI	Human Development Index
HRBA	Human Rights Based Approach
ICT	Information and Communication Technology
ICT4D	Information and Communication Technology for Development
IMED	Internal Monitoring and Evaluation Division
LFM	Logical Framework Matrix
LGRD	Local Government and Rural Development
LGED	Local Government Engineering Division

LGIs	Local Government Institutions
M&E	Monitoring and Evaluation
MDG	Millennium Development Goal
MLAA	Madaripur Legal Aid Association
MoA	Ministry of Agriculture
MoF	Ministry of Finance
MoHFW	Ministry of Health and Family Welfare
MoWCA	Ministry of Women and Children Affairs
NAPD	National Academy for Planning and Development
NGOAB	NGO Affairs Bureau
NGO	Nongovernmental Organisation
NILG	National Institute for Local Government
NPM	New Public Management
OECD	Organisation for Economic Cooperation and Development
PKSF	Palli Karma-Sahayak Foundation
PPRC	Power and Participation Research Centre
RDA	Rural Development Academy
RDRS	Rangpur Dinajpur Rural Service
RMG	Readymade garments
SDG	Sustainable Development Goal
TA	Technical Assistance
TAPP	Technical Assistance Project Proforma
TIB	Transparency International Bangladesh
UCEP	Underprivileged Children Education Program
UISC	Union Information Service Centre
UH&FPO	UPZ Health and Family Planning officer
UN	United Nations
UNDP	United Nations Development Program
UNO	UPZ Nirbahi (Executive) Officer
UP	Union Parishad (council)
UPZ	Upazila (sub-districts)
WB	World Bank
WBG	World Bank Group

CHAPTER ONE

UNPACKING THE QUEST

Introduction

It is difficult to find any development literature that does not discuss people, given that the concept in itself is about people and their participation. The government in any given country routinely undertakes development initiatives that are designed for and delivered to its citizens. In turn, citizens are expected to be involved in conveying their opinions appropriately, take part in implementing developmental activities, provide feedback on how they benefit from development, and continue with the benefits they receive from these initiatives. This broad understanding of development is narrowed by projects at the micro-level, where participation of target beneficiaries in individual ventures seems to be an integral part of project management. Discussions on development also argue that governments do not wish to pursue development alone but instead partner with nongovernment organisations (NGOs) to respond to their policy advocacy and ensure its intended services reach the people in need. Development practitioners in both sectors are likewise encouraged to dedicate great efforts to ensuring that developmental decisions come from people (or beneficiaries at the micro level) engaged in the process, and who can thus contribute at both local and national levels.

However, one question remains unanswered: How are people participating in the development process, and what roles, experiences and strategies are relevant for government organisations (GOs) and NGOs in the pursuit of development participation? Within the context of Bangladesh, it proved additionally important to identify the factors that stimulate or influence these organisations to ensure that people do participate in the process of managing development initiatives. Based on fieldwork conducted for the PhD study,[1] specific queries answered in this book are related to: factors of influence from government policy and development

[1] Background provided in Acknowledgement. The study was conducted from February 2013 to December 2019.

partners; how engaging beneficiaries leads to development participation; when NGOs are perceived as essential for ensuring people's participation, if GOs are equally responsible (and capable); and gauging the understanding (if any) between government and NGO entities working to bring people closer to development.

Bangladesh has experienced steady and continuous improvement in economic growth, with local government effecting development programs and policies to include non-state actors (NGOs, private sectors). The public-sector development planning and policies are focused on delivering services to people, interacting with rural people, undertaking rural and infrastructural development, integrating women in national expansion, and achieving and sustaining the UN Millennium Development Goals (MDGs). Also noted was the country's transformation from "disaster victim" to "disaster manager," and from a food-deficit nation of 70 million people to a "nearly self-sufficient" country of 168.22 million (BBS 2021), bringing "abroad" home through exports and expats, and connecting "isolated villages" to a "national economy" (PPRC 2016, 3). Along with the public sector, the key players contributing to the country's development include private sectors, NGOs and development partners. Bangladesh is likewise renowned for its various microfinancing models led by the Grameen Bank, Bangladesh Rural Advancement Committee (BRAC), the Association of Social Advancements (ASA) and other leading NGOs working in various sectors. The private sector is equally responsible for contributing to the country's gradual economic development through readymade garment (RMG) exports, remittances from overseas employment, and private-sector investments and industries. Bangladesh targets becoming an upper middle-income country by 2031 and a higher-income country by 2041 according to an overall scenario of a foreign-assistance management report of 2021–2 by the Economic Relations Division [ERD] (n. d.).

The country's development planning over five financial years (FY) forecasts growth relative to its Annual Development Program (ADP) budget allocation. Along with the government's allowance for the ADP, Bangladesh also receives project aid in the form of grants and loans (ERD 2012). Project aid is integral to the country as it finances ADPs related to human-resource development; social, health, educational and family welfare; as well as infrastructural development (Raihan 2012, 250). The Government of Bangladesh (GOB) is responsible for undertaking development programs. However, NGOs also manage development projects in various service sectors, as either implementing partners to the government or independent providers of services, skills and advocacy as approved by the relevant government authority. Government line ministries, departments and field administrations are further held accountable for undertaking development initiatives and delivering services to people. NGOs generally implement development projects, receiving funds from development partners and the GOB, and operating within legal and administrative policy frameworks. Naturally, each has financial and administrative accountability to their respective authorities, including line ministries, departments and the NGO Affairs Bureau (NGOAB), as applicable within the national context. Table 1.1 presents a snapshot of the country context.

Table 1.1. The research context: Bangladesh

Political context
• The People's Republic of Bangladesh established on December 16, 1971 following its victory in the nine-month liberation war with Pakistan
• Change from parliamentary to presidential form of government in 1973
• Long-term military regime from 1975 to 1990
• Mass movement against military regime in 1990
• General election in 1991 and return to democracy with the parliamentary form of government
• Change of government through general elections, maintaining a parliamentary democracy from 1991 to date.
Geographic context (BBS 2022)
• Area 147,570 km^2
• Generally plain land with hilly terrain in a couple of districts in Sylhet and Chittagong divisions
• Borders with: o India to the north and west o The Bay of Bengal to the south o India and Myanmar to the east
Development context in brief (BBS 2022), WB Country Data (online), ERD (n. d.)
• Experienced end of war in 1971; natural disasters and famine immediately after independence
• Steady economic growth of GDP from (-)14% in 1972 to 6.9% in 2021; GDP: USD 416 billion
• Per-capita income USD 2,591 in 2020–1

• MDG achievements in poverty reduction, girl child education, reducing child mortality rate and ensuring child and maternity health
• Foreign assistance: 56% multilateral and 44% bilateral commitments in FY 2021–2
• Private-sector investment of GDP: 23.70% in FY 2020–1
• Share of RMG in national export: 81.16% in FY 2020–1
• Received remittances: BDT 2,101.31 billion in FY 2020–1
• Grant disbursement stands at 1.97% and loan disbursement at 98.03% in FY 2021–2
• Total electricity generation in FY 2020–1 stands at 80,423 MKWh
• Development priorities: agriculture and rural development, industry, energy, transport, human-resources development, population planning, education and training, health and sanitation, nutrition and food safety, ICT and telecommunication, infrastructural development
People context (BBS 2022)
• Total population: 168.22 m
• Literacy rate: 75.2%
• Language: Bangla (Bengali)
Administrative units (BBS 2022)
• 8 divisions, 64 districts, 12 city corporations, 330 municipalities, 495 Upazilas[2] (UPZ), 4,571 Union Parishads[3] (UPs)

Although they play a significant role in the country's development, GOs and NGOs are criticised on various fronts, particularly for the lack of accountability to development beneficiaries, a preference for donors to provide foreign aid directly to NGOs, and NGO agreements for donor conditionality. Conversely, there is inadequate coordination between the GOs and NGOs in implementing development programs, top-down decision making in the public sector, and governmental control over NGO activities which are commonly attributed to GOs.

However, none of these issues has yet led to any critical discussions on how development is integrating people, what roles GOs and NGOs play in connecting people, and whether people are integrated into the country's

[2] Sub-districts; there are Upazilas under each district.

[3] Union councils, a local-government body at the rural level under the Ministry of LGRD.

development process. The extent to which the policies of these organisations are inclusive of their people remains unclear, and the leveraging within their partnership, geared to ensure people are engaged in development, is yet to receive critical attention. These gaps certainly create an opportunity for this book to illustrate how development participation is achieved in a specific country context such as Bangladesh. To this end, the book reflects the two main areas of development discourse: first, the conceptual framework and organisational roles of state and non-state actors that are expected to involve people in national-development initiatives; and second, the process of integrating people into the development process.

Development concepts have been evolving since the 1940s, focusing on economic development, poverty reduction, decentralisation and the participation of non-state actors and people to ensure inclusive, participatory and people-centred development. In the practical applications of theories and concepts, it is the country and people contexts that determine participation achievements. In the Bangladesh context, how beneficiaries are engaged determines how much they participate in the development process, and their reception of and response to development interventions largely impact that participation.

Development Participation: The Background

Development is a contested concept; despite numerous critiques, it has been accepted globally, and governments consider development as a basis for ensuring continuous improvement in people's lives. Thus, development is undeniable, be it a success or failure for a country that works to improve a specific condition, such as poverty (Rist 2007). The concept is also a paradox, as explained by Kothari and Minogue (2002). To some it means imperialism: it creates a direct dependence on the developed world and is a result of colonisation. The Western developed countries thought that exiting once-colonised countries would create a vacuum they could fill through assistance while not ruling directly (Kohli 1986). This circumstance reflects the dependency of an underdeveloped nation on developed nations' aid, where reliance eventually manifests in policymaking and domestic rule begins to reflect foreign interests (Spivak 1999; Smith 1986; Kentor and Boswell 2003; Escobar 2010). Reflecting on development in the West for countries below the thresholds of income, economy and development (as standardised by the UN and OECD glossary) opened debates concerning developing-world dependency on the developed world. These debates suggest that the former is expected to follow the latter's lead due to the developed world's comparatively overwhelming economic power and political influence. It is said that dependency on aid causes resources to flow from underdeveloped to developed countries in the name of development (Willis 2011, 79).[4] Crush's (1995) notion of the colonial influence of development connects it closely with geography, dividing the world between developed countries bursting with resources and systems, and underdeveloped countries lacking capital and desperate for development. Evidently, development has little "conviction and coherence" if it is not related to geography and does not further promote ideas about developed and underdeveloped regions of the world (Crush 1995, 550).

These criticisms of colonisation and dependency give rise to the concept of "decolonised" development on the basis that difference should be considered and the local context duly addressed, as well as local actions valued. In this regard, "decolonisation" is further defined as a "self-reflexive collective practice in the transformation of the self, reconceptualization of identity and political mobilization" – all of which Mohanty (2003, 8) deems necessary in encouraging the process. Further, the concept involves engagement with everyday issues and various social groups, "premised on ideas of autonomy and self-determination" as well as "democratic practice" (Mohanty 2003, 254). Similar arguments are given by Sabaratnam (2017, as cited in Buba 2019), who outlines a need to decolonise development assistance and engage more with the targets (i.e. the people or beneficiaries of development) by considering the reality of their conditions. Thus, development is defined as "an idea, an objective and an activity," with related questions being "for whom and whose development" and what activities are included (Kothari and Minogue 2002, 12). For Rist (2007, 488), development should be defined as "actual social practices and their consequences," which anyone can identify. Development practice is expected to have a "human side," which has been missing in achieving economic growth (Campbell and Hoyle 1990, 6–7). The notion of "progress-based development" that emerged in the 1960s failed to provide solutions to alleviate poverty and instead created disillusionment among theorists and practitioners, leading to the concept of developmental aid for the rural poor (Shams 1990, 222). To address this "human side," development approaches had to shift their focus towards integrating rural development that could address the "human" needs of even the poorest groups. This approach extended to providing access to social services such as health, education, nutrition, family planning and employee productivity, instead of purely economic growth (Rondinelli 1986, 112–13). The International

[4] The author imagines a structure that outlines the dependency of peripheral entities (i.e. recipients of development assistance) on core entities (i.e. providers of development assistance).

Labour Organization, United National Development Programme (UNDP) and the World Bank (WB) played vital roles in emphasising the "urgent and necessary" need to directly target the globe's more disadvantaged regions (Riddell 2007, 32). Hence, resolving to address the "human side" of development added a new dimension to the development concept, which was certainly nurtured at organisations funnelling developmental aid to underdeveloped countries.

With this focus on the human side, the theories and concepts shifted towards development participation. People, for whom the development is planned and implemented, should influence the development activities through empowerment, capacity building and cost sharing.[5] Chambers (1984, 12) argued in favour of "putting people first," taking community-based development and combining professionalism with the endogenous knowledge rural people possess. This concept of putting people at the centre of development discourse also led to questions of whose voice counts and where the responsibility lies in bringing change – from economic growth to community participation (Holland and Blackburn 1998). Illustrating the philosophy of "people-based" development and how the concept of beneficiary participation emerged, Oakley and Marsden (1984, 11, 25, 28) maintain that organisational structures could provide rural people with avenues of "contact with and a voice in development programs" necessary to mobilise and empower them to "determine which needs, and whose needs will be met through the distribution of resources." This requires the mobilisation of people, which has an effect on those who need to minimise their normal work in order to participate in the development programs, which is why it is called a "tyranny" (Cooke and Kothari 2001). That said, participation is said to be transformational, as illustrated by Hickey and Mohan (2001). In analysing community involvement, the development literature typically prioritises locals to minimise the "mismatch" between community perceptions and practises, as well as outsider policies (Gujja, Pimbert and Shah 1998, 60). The role of the government in integrating people into development was further emphasised with the concept of New Public Management (NPM), minimising the gaps between the state, non-state actors and people, placing the markets ahead of the government (Steger and Roy 2010; Boston 2011; Apeldoorn and Overbeek 2012). Following the emergence of NPM, people became the customers of the public service in many developed countries (Jamil 2002). Thus, state (public-sector) and non-

[5] Paul (1987) identified that the WB mainstreamed public engagement in 38% of its projects.

state actors (NGOs, private-sector) were deemed essential to addressing people's demands in the development.

People-oriented development found new dimension in the work of Nobel Laureate Amartya Sen. His book *Development as Freedom* (1999) established connections between the development achieved and the freedom people possessed as outcomes of growth. His concept of development as "freedom" opposes "unfreedom," in which individuals cannot have or sustain the benefits of development if they, for example, are bound by hunger, encounter child mortality, are deprived of political rights or are denied access to social services. According to this understanding of development as akin to freedom, various processes and opportunities must be in place for people to participate in their prospective growth, which Corbridge (2002) considers as the existence of "geographical space" in linking development and "freedom." Essentially, this space differs according to physical location and whether governments are authoritarian or democratic. The author is further critical of denoting a straightforward relationship between both forms of rule when measuring development as freedom. He finds that "true development" involves the "active participation of informed human beings in the processes of social change" (Corbridge 2002, 191). This concept of linking "informed" people to development certainly creates an opportunity to examine the strategies available for engagement in the process, through which people are informed and capable of understanding the benefits in a specific country context.

The beginning of the new millennium saw a declaration to achieve MDGs by 2015. This comprehensive focus on development reinforced the importance of creating people-centred development goals. The creation of the Millennium Declaration in 2000 soon recognised the need for a "collective responsibility to uphold the principles of human dignity, equality and equity at the global level," and further clarified the duty for world leaders (if they are donors, governments or heads of states) to honour the "world's people" (UN n. d.). Indeed, the Millennium Declaration alerted the attention of development organisations and practitioners to individual importance in achieving the MDGs. For Fukuda-Parr (2004, 396), these goals put "human development, poverty, people and their lives" at the centre of the global-development agenda, measuring "human wellbeing rather than economic growth," with development adding a different dimension that is "human." The role of people in relation to development was reiterated in the Sustainable Development Goals (SDGs) adopted at the UN Sustainable Development Summit in 2015. Kumar, Kumar and Vivekadhish (2016, 2) categorise these goals into three groups covering inclusiveness, sustainability for future generations, and their function in extending the MDGs. Table 1.2

summarises the gradual progression of development concepts in practise focusing on people, evolving at the international level and passed on to countries bound by treaties and declarations.

Table 1.2. Development initiatives and focus on people (1940s to date)

International initiatives	Development focus and people orientation
UN Charter 1945	Social progress for people; better standards of life, fundamental freedoms; excludes "distinction as to race, sex, language, or religion"
Universal Declaration on Human Rights 1948	Universal protection of fundamental human rights, entitlement of rights and freedom
Economic development in 1950s	Assistance to underdeveloped countries in South and Southeast Asia
Formation of Development Assistance Committee, Organisation for Economic Cooperation and Development (OECD) in 1960s	Consultation among donors and assistance to less developed countries; private investment in developing countries
Common Aid Effort in 1961	Improving people's standard of life; assisting less developed countries to improve their economies
Establishment of Official Development Assistance 1970	Economic and social development of developing countries
Development Cooperation in 1970s	Poverty reduction agenda; rural development
Aid Coordination in 1980s	Effectiveness of aid provided to developing countries; structural adjustment; policy making in aid-recipient countries; project appraisal comprising identification, selection, design, monitoring and evaluation
Development cooperation in 1990s	People's participation in the development process; democratic government, market and private-sector development
MDGs in 2000	Governments, international community, civil society and private sector working together to achieve development goals centred on people and their development
SDGs in 2015	Peace and prosperity for people and the planet

Source: adapted from Dutta (2021a), based on Führer (1996), UN (n. d.) and UNDP (n. d.)

The conceptual frameworks of development and participation, though contested, form the basis for development assistance and the strategies undertaken at the international and national levels. Notably, the High Level Forum on Harmonisation held in Rome in 2003, the 2005 Paris Declaration on Aid Effectiveness and the 2008 Accra Agenda on Action provide key examples of initiatives highlighting the need for improved coordination at the national level. These coordination efforts extend to increased donor and partner countries' respective accountability to their nations' citizens, and efforts to translate development actions into positive change in people's lives. However, increased focus on the procedures, results and effect of developmental assistance and aid coordination meant less attention was given to beneficiaries regarding human rights, social justice and equity (Kelegama 2012, 3). Sjöstedt (2013) argues that the Paris Declaration in particular focuses on the priorities of partner countries, results reporting and prioritising development on behalf of donors. It seems that MDG achievements are geared more towards reaching targets than generating discussions around how people form the basis of developmental success.

Engaging Beneficiaries for Development Participation: The Gap

Evidently, people have been at the centre of development discussions. However, their integration into the process has not yet been interpreted through the evolution of "engagement" as a concept. Engagement is linked with people's participation in development, which has progressed over several decades. The concept of engaging beneficiaries is less evident in these development concepts; instead, the literature has progressed with the concept of people's participation in development, and its methods, problems and challenges. While development concepts focus on people and their participation, illustrating participation through a beneficiary lens is limited in the development field. Krull (1999, 6) identified popular participation in development programs, defining it as the "voluntary dedication of resources with an expectation of future benefits." Thus, concepts of development participation imply that beneficiaries will actively participate in decision-making, influencing and providing direction in the implementation of development programs and sharing the benefits (Krull 1999). The participatory approach to development concepts argues for this approach. Theoretically, this approach means allowing communities in rural settings to identify problems, plan projects and assist with implementation (Lunt et al. 2018), either by decision-making or resource sharing.

That said, people (or, more specifically, development beneficiaries) may employ "participation calculus" to compare the time and efforts demanded of participation against the potential benefits they expect in return; through this consideration, they can choose whether their involvement will "accrue" to them (Awortwi 2013, 91). "Participation calculus" confers the expectations that beneficiaries have of their involvement in development. Expectations are the critical factors that organisations must address when managing development projects, demanding proper management of ability and expectation upon engagement. According to Purvis, Zagenczyk and McCray (2015, 3), the most important determinant of stakeholder participation lies within one's self-interests,[6] and this is equally true for beneficiaries, as they are the key stakeholders of the development interventions. People may also need adequate freedom to feel confident enough to be involved, or otherwise the engagement process requires greater facilitation for wider involvement. Awortwi (2013) identified that not all communities for whom interventions are undertaken become involved. Thus, the organisational setting (GOs and NGOs in this book) is necessary for conveying development benefits, facilitating beneficiary understanding of the development initiatives, and creating opportunities for the active involvement of beneficiaries (Purvis, Zagenczyk and McCray 2015; Helfer 2006; Sillitoe 2000). Having strategies in place that meet the requisite demands proves essential, as approaches to securing beneficiary participation "across different cultural settings" are inherently "framed" and "operate" according to circumstance (Kenny 2016, 34; Stone 1989).

Lukensmeyer and Torres (2006, 7, 9) distinguish "citizen engagement" from "citizen participation," and define "engagement" as working directly with people throughout a "process" to understand their "concerns and aspirations," which are "consistently understood and considered" in institutional decision making. They add that, in whatever form people are engaged, the purpose is to "recognize and build upon a fundamental right of all citizens to have a say in the decisions that affect their lives." In identifying the problems of participation and suggesting ways to "remake" participation, Eversole (2010) explains participation as an attempt to engage others in decision making, noting that its eventual management and funding are subject to organisational control. Thus "engagement" can be viewed as a process that encourages participation but requires equal facilitation from professional organisations as well as resource support (Eversole 2010).

All these definitions of engaging people in development as beneficiaries describe a process that this book has identified in the Bangladesh context.

---

[6] Self-interests of beneficiaries, organisations and other stakeholders.

Beneficiary engagement also falls under the broad conceptual framework of "stakeholder engagement," which is inextricably linked to most development practises. Taylor (2002, 125) notes its influence on private sectors promoting managerialism in developed countries, eventually spreading to GOs and NGOs in developing countries. According to the WBG (2018) report, multistakeholder engagement began in the 1970s, was formalised in the 1980s and subsequently deepened throughout the 1990s through participatory approaches in various operations; in turn, these efforts reiterated the benefit of recognising citizens' inputs. It is important to note that beneficiaries are not the only stakeholders involved in development, but are part of a whole range of stakeholders in a specific development intervention. Thus, articulating beneficiary engagement through the stakeholder-engagement process is inadequate for illustrating how, when and to what extent beneficiaries are engaged in a specific development context.

Given this interconnection between beneficiary engagement and development participation, the concept of beneficiary engagement has evolved as "people-oriented" development theories have needed to illustrate the conditioning factors under which people (the beneficiaries at the local level) participate. The above findings from literture still require an examination of the context for how and when beneficiaries are engaged to participate in the development process. Also essential to understanding development participation and beneficiary engagement is an understanding of the stimulating factors for beneficiaries getting engaged and eventually participating. This book addresses these gaps in understanding, examining these queries from the viewpoints of GOs, NGOs, development practitioners and beneficiaries in Bangladesh.

Against this backdrop, the book examines beneficiary engagement specific to the development context of Bangladesh by reviewing existing development practises and GO–NGO scopes in engaging beneficiaries. In this context, the book identifies that the scope of beneficiary engagement is embedded in both government and NGO development planning and policies which supplement each other to achieve participation. However, engaging beneficiaries for their participation largely depends on how they receive and respond to development interventions. To this end, organisational infrastructure such as GOs or NGOs and development projects are instrumental in transferring policies into practises and engaging beneficiaries that ultimately results in their participation. It is interesting to discover that engaging beneficiaries is incubated by the development projects[7] which GOs and NGOs undertake and implement at the field level. Different phases of

---

[7] The term "project" is defined later in this chapter.

project management affect beneficiary engagement differently, though the implementation phase covers the largest part of it. Beneficiary engagement is related to a development project in terms of management, personnel, GO–NGO implementation, project templates, service delivery and funding. It requires ongoing interactions with beneficiaries to engage them with the expected outcome of their participation in the development process, identified in this book.

This book reveals that both GOs and NGOs experience challenges and advantages in engaging beneficiaries. Illustrating these challenges and advantages creates an opportunity to observe the extent to which beneficiaries are engaged in the development process. Although the GO–NGO relationship in Bangladesh has been defined as complex because of a lack of coordination and bureaucratic control, the book argues that none of these organisations has absolute leverage to engage beneficiaries without the support of each other in the development field. The existing GO–NGO relationship in Bangladesh is more about coordination than conflicts. Challenges also include new development thrusts, emerging private sectors and mega-projects narrowing the scope of beneficiary engagement. However, the partnership between GOs and NGOs is desirable for minimising challenges and enhancing beneficiary engagement in development. New development opportunities are emerging that can create more scope for GOs and NGOs to engage beneficiaries, ensuring their participation in the process.

Terminologies

As the discussion progresses, reference to specific terminologies helps retain focus on the book's aims and objectives. Thus, key terms are defined in this section to provide an understanding and further clarify their use in chapter discussions. These terms are commonly used in the literature on development administration, international cooperation, project design and implementation. However, defining these terms specifically for this book is essential in elucidating their connection within the country context.

Engaging

This term is used to demonstrate how people are involved in development initiatives that either the GOs or NGOs undertake in Bangladesh. "Engaging" with development initiatives includes receiving and responding to information about them and understanding how they will affect the lives and livelihoods of beneficiaries. This book identifies that engaging is a way to ensure beneficiary participation in the development process. This terminology is based on several definitions of "engaging" identified earlier in this chapter and when investigating the research questions for the study. To keep the key theme clear, the term "beneficiary engagement" is abbreviated to BE.

Beneficiaries

Development deals with beneficiaries at a micro-level and citizens at a macro level, with projects residing in the former relative to development (Gaventa and Valderrama 1999). In this view, the term "beneficiaries" refers to the recipients of development interventions in any given context, including those associated with receiving services through development projects and from GOs, NGOs and local-government institutions. The term "beneficiaries" refers to both men and women at the project setting and participating in the wider development context. In the context of the study, beneficiaries also represent research participants who were interviewed and participated in the focus-group discussion.

Development

Instead of measuring the statistical scale of progress or financial growth, the term "development" is used as a basis for projects through which the government and NGOs in Bangladesh undertake initiatives to improve beneficiary conditions. In this book it suggests improving conditions (e.g. livelihood, education, social and economic conditions), empowering and building capacity for participation as relevant to Bangladesh. Bangladesh is called a "developing country" based on the categories identified by Willis (2011, 16–19), and illustrated in Fig 1.1.

Fig. 1.1. Categories of developed and developing countries

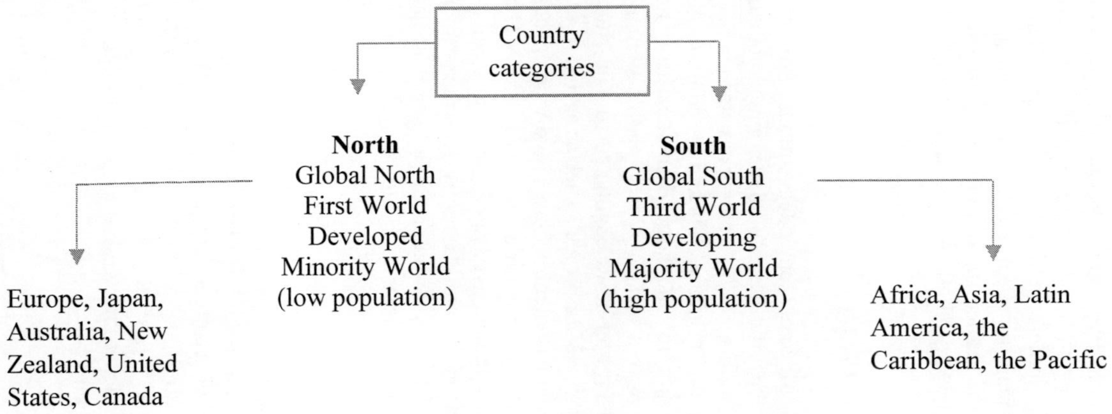

Source: Dutta (2021a)

Development participation

As identified in the literature discussed earlier, development participation suggests that beneficiaries actively and/or voluntarily participate in development interventions. They influence the planning of programs by identifying problems, guiding implementation and sharing resources and benefits of the development meant for them. Development participation is linked to BE, considering that the former cannot follow any specific strategy and needs to adapt to the contexts or challenges as they occur (Lunt et al. 2018).

Projects

Projects comprise the specific development interventions through which agents implement policies in specific areas of development planning in Bangladesh. Herein, "project"[8] refers to development assistance undertaken by the government or NGOs in the service sectors and the community about the capacity development meant for the target beneficiaries. The term "project" helps narrow the focus to a specific area of people's engagement in development, as identified in interviews conducted for the study. The focus is on engagement in service-sector projects such as agriculture, health or education, and other social-development ventures involving capacity and service delivery within specific communities in rural areas. The term "project" in this book refers to technical assistance (TA) and service-sector projects where both GOs and NGOs work directly with beneficiaries. It excludes any infrastructural, capital investment or industrial projects, as NGOs are not involved in these endeavours in Bangladesh.[9]

Government Organisations (GOs)

The Government of Bangladesh consists of three branches: Executive, Legislative and Judiciary. The term "GOs" refers to the Executive branch (incorporating line ministries, departments and service sectors) and field administration, comprising divisions, districts, Upazilas and Union Parishads. Throughout the book, "GOs" denotes any of these organisations and their representative respondents interviewed or participating in focus-group discussions during fieldwork.

---

[8] See Appendix A. According to the Planning Commission (GOB 2016, 1–22) under the Ministry of Planning, projects are divided into seven categories.
[9] See Appendix A for definitions of different types of projects.

Nongovernment Organisations (NGOs)

The term "NGOs" refers to registered entities that fall within the definition provided in the Foreign Donation (Voluntary Activities) Regulations Act 2016 of Bangladesh. Under this Act, NGOs are deemed voluntary bodies registered by the Department of Social Services working within Bangladesh at the field level, local agents receiving foreign funding, and foreign voluntary organisations that are registered by the NGO Affairs Bureau (NGOAB) which operates under the authority of the Prime Minister's office. The term also includes respondents from NGOs.

Methodology

Qualitative methods were followed to gather data and illustrate the topic of this book. This methodology employs first-hand understanding to inform analysis (Silverman 2004, 37). Qualitative methods seek answers to research questions by "examining various social settings and the individuals who inhabit these settings" (Bryman 2008; Berg 2004). Moreover, qualitative studies have proved essential for obtaining full insight into relevant organisations and communicating with research participants during fieldwork. The qualitative approach helps to establish contact with the key officials responsible for project implementation, follow policies and procedures, and engage beneficiaries and evaluate the deliverables, all of which occur within complex settings involving multiple stakeholders. Qualitative methods also help to examine the framework in which GOs and NGOs operate, which demands a total understanding of the subject matter.

The qualitative-data-collection approach helped to generate a detailed investigation through interviews with forty-two respondents from GOs, NGOs, beneficiaries, project personnel, fieldworkers and development partners. Interviewees included sixteen respondents from GOs, eleven from NGOs, five from project management, three from development partners, five beneficiaries, one private-sector respondent related to the agriculture-development program, and one journalist working for an online newspaper. In addition, three separate focus-group discussions (FGDs) with GOs, NGOs and beneficiaries were held during the fieldwork, adding thirty-seven participants from these groups. Research participants were selected following a purposive sampling process considering their relevance, roles and experiences related to the research topic, as mentioned in Table 1.3. Participant selection was predetermined by the research questions and according to the contextual relevance in relation to each institution's

Table 1.3. Predetermined factors for purposive sampling

Predetermined criteria to select research participants		Profile of data samples				
	Categories of respondents	GOs	NGOs	Development partners	Project Beneficiaries	Project-management staff
	Research participants	Public servants and managers at the centre, district, sub-district and union levels	Executives Fieldworkers Project managers	Officials working in bilateral and multilateral agencies in Bangladesh or relevant organisations	Project participants/ beneficiaries	Project managers Development practitioners Evaluation officers
	Perceived roles	Decide development initiatives, provide public services to citizens, accountable for public expenditure	Implement projects, deliver project outputs, work with beneficiaries, report to government and donors	Decide on project funding at international and national levels	Service recipients, Entrepreneurs, Users of project outputs, Community representatives	Oversee project implementation, interact with beneficiaries and project stakeholders, report, implement projects

Source: (Dutta 2021a)

strategic functions.[10] Interviews and FGDs were held at different levels: district, UPZ and UP.

The study that this book is based on obtained required approval from the University of Canberra's Human Research Ethics Committee (HREC). After a rigorous review process, the study obtained HREC approval on December 8, 2014 (Project No. 14-243), with the data-collection period granted until December 31, 2017. All data were gathered during the approved period. Each interview and FGD was carried out through obtaining the participant's consent in writing. To maintain participants' privacy, their details are not disclosed, as required by the university's research ethics policy. Semi-structured interviews were conducted to gauge the perceptions and roles of the government and NGO officials, fieldworkers and project personnel responsible at different levels for interacting with the beneficiaries. Secondary data sources were consulted to better understand the existing policies and development planning in Bangladesh, and to crosscheck information obtained following discussions. These sources included:

- several five-year plans (FYPs), Vision 2021, Perspective Plan
- ADP and ERD (Economic Relations Division) Reports
- government policies on development assistance and relations to bilateral and multilateral-development partners
- the National Policy of Agriculture
- the National Agricultural Extension Policy
- the Primary Health Care Policy
- government policies on NGO governance
- policies on primary education
- Women Development policies
- NGO policies
- the Local Government (Union Parishad) Act 2009 and Planning Rules 2013
- international treaties, declarations and organisational policies for development cooperation

Secondary data corresponded to the qualitative nature of the study, as well as the selection and application of a mixed-method approach to analysis. It proved necessary for gathering official facts and figures concerning the investigation in this book. It is important to note that these documents were available on Bangladesh government portals under

[10] GOs and NGOs, beneficiaries, project staff and bilateral and multilateral agencies funding development initiatives.

different ministries and departments. Secondary sources available in the public domain and on websites were consulted and are duly referenced in the bibliography. Documents or references not available in the public domain were not considered for discussion in this book.

Essentially, FGDs helped in understanding participants' experiences within both government and nongovernment spheres. Dialogue through FGDs proved especially critical, including dialogue with GOs working in different government capacities, fieldworkers and project staff working in various NGOs, and project beneficiaries receiving government and nongovernment services and development benefits. FGDs, with GO and NGO officials, helped gather perspectives from individual standpoints and within organisational contexts relating to policy, procedure and practical experiences in engaging beneficiaries. There were not significant constraints on obtaining data; however, arranging interviews and FGDs was challenging due to the time constraints of the research participants. In addition, the fieldwork required several trips to and from Bangladesh and internal travels to district UPZs and UPs. No resistance to interviews was experienced, though two interviews had to be abandoned as the participants did not participate (no reason was stated), despite signing the consent forms. These two consent forms were deducted from the total number of interviews.

Thematic coding, interpretation of the findings and document analysis were used to examine data from interviews, FGDs and secondary sources. Document analysis was used mainly to analyse data from official statistics, policies, reports and acts or laws, as applicable. The book does not contain any significant quantitative data analysis. The approach of analysing primary and secondary data sources further helped to triangulate and crosscheck information sourced from interviews, FGDs and relevant documents. The book also includes some graphical representation of information prepared using the qualitative-data analysis software NVivo Pro 11.

Overview of Contents

This book is divided into six chapters, with supporting appendices. The following sections provide brief descriptions of each chapter, including a general overview of how the book is structured.

Chapter one outlines the background, development concepts and gap prevailing for BE and participation in the development literature. It is important to understand the concepts of development participation and BE, and the background provided in this chapter helps to understand the analysis in the Bangladesh context. In addition, the conceptual gap mentioned in this chapter justifies the research findings and analysis. The chapter also provides an overview of how the analysis progresses and includes definitions of the terminology used and the methodology followed.

Chapter two explores the basis for BE perceived by GOs, NGOs, beneficiaries and project personnel interviewed and participating in FGDs. How they understand the terminology is focused on people, though this varies when referring to beneficiaries and approaches to development participation in the Bangladesh context. While GOs cover a wide range of beneficiaries, NGOs are limited to the specific target groups they work with. The chapter discusses how the concept of BE is integrated into public and NGO sectors, although with different connotations, as is evident in the literature and research findings. Given the organisational basis for BE identified during fieldwork, this chapter presents the contexts of BE as currently perceived, along with strategies to transfer policies into practises for engaging beneficiaries within public and NGO sectors.

Chapter three identifies how development participation and its orientation towards people have been integrated into government and NGO development initiatives driven by their respective development planning and projects. The chapter discusses how development projects, in which beneficiary interactions within organisations occur, seem to be instrumental in transferring these policies into practice. It reveals that specific components of BE in the project – compliance with project manuals and templates, beneficiary interactions on the planning and evaluation of projects, and communicating the benefits – lead to BE for development participation. This chapter also demonstrates how beneficiaries receive and respond to development communication, which enables organisations to engage them within project settings. In brief, BE occurs within project settings which are impacted by various factors, and as such, development participation is not straightforward.

Chapter four analyses the comparative advantages and limitations of GO–NGO practises which affect BE. It reveals that the presence and absence of certain factors impact BE, revealing the extent to which beneficiaries participate in the development field. To this end, GOs and NGOs experience advantages and limitations in engaging beneficiaries. Instead of one leveraging over the other, this chapter argues that an individual entity utilises the advantages of the other when it is required for BE to ensure participation rather than generate conflicts.

Given this interdependence between GOs and NGOs, the analysis in chapter five reveals that existing partnerships between these two entities aimed at engaging beneficiaries have emergent opportunities and challenges that impact their bond and improve local involvement. This chapter argues that coordination between GOs and NGOs is the desired condition, and the complementarity of the relationship seems instrumental in enhancing BE. It also reveals the emerging development trends in Bangladesh for which BE is essential to upscaling development participation.

The final chapter concludes the discussion by summing up how BE leads to development participation, and in what context it occurs. The chapter raises a few concerns in relation to the future of development participation in the absence of enabling factors which determine the extent to which development participation is achieved through BE.

CHAPTER TWO

THE BASIS FOR ENGAGING BENEFICIARIES

The broad spectrum of development, participation and engaging beneficiaries, as discussed in the previous chapter, creates a scope for understanding how people-oriented development and the roles of GOs and NGOs are outlined in practice for BE in the development context of Bangladesh. The people orientation of the government's development planning creates scopes for NGOs to align their objectives with GOs. That said, understanding and perception of the terminology by GOs, NGOs, beneficiaries and practitioners are related to BE in practice. In addition, donor conditions play a critical role for BE in development planning and implementation in the government and NGO development initiatives. Transferring policies into practises for BE follows project implementation, along with several other factors that are essential in the Bangladesh context to orient people with development, which the development concepts have been advocating for several decades.

Engaging Beneficiaries: A Varied Understanding

Background information will better inform the coming judgements regarding how the government and NGO officials have addressed the idea of engaging beneficiaries in practice. Further discussed is how participants from other respondent groups (following interviews) perceive BE. This compiles the various knowledge bases that each of the research participants shared regarding individual-level involvement within both policy and project management in the development context of Bangladesh. Identifying different understandings of the terminology helped to connect organisational approaches to BE in the same context.

BE from the Government and NGO Perspectives

While collecting data through FGDs with GOs and NGOs, participants generated discussion on who their beneficiaries are and how they conceptualise the term "engagement" within their development context.

Table 2.1 provides an overview of FGD data detailing GO–NGO perspectives on what "engagement" means in the daily practice of development and implementing development interventions.

Table 2.1. What does "engagement" mean to GOs and NGOs?

GOs on BE	**NGOs on BE**
Implementers	Inclusion
People	Participation
Regulators	Sharing
Policymakers	Relation
Financer	Information
Attach	Community and Village Association
Agreeing	Credibility of information
Involving	Correct information
Taking on board	Timely information
Contractor	Job responsibility of engaging beneficiaries
Children	Accountability to beneficiaries
Women	Commitment to need-based claim
Farmers	Evaluation
Stakeholders	Monitoring
Fishermen	Align
Involving	

It is interesting to note in Table 2.1 that the responses from GOs were relatively more focused on processes and institutional responsibilities when addressing engagement. In contrast, NGOs aligned more with hands-on engagement practises, as shown in Figs. 2.1 and 2.2.

Fig. 2.1. GOs' responses to BE

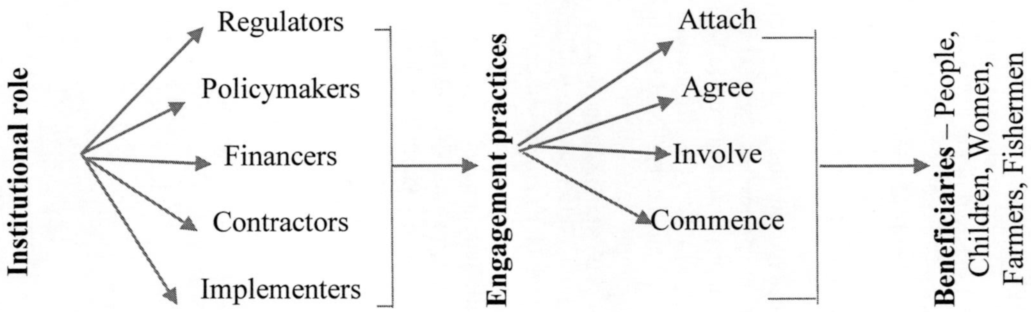

Source: based on Dutta (2021a)

According to what participants expressed, active involvement necessitates ongoing attempts to link different institutions (from policy formulation to implementation) with multiple dimensions perceived as instrumental to local-level engagement. Thus, GOs tend to focus on the various concepts on and around individual engagement and the factors that precede its formation, such as policies and regulations, finance, and implementers and contractors. From the government perspective, target beneficiaries are from all social, cultural and economic walks of life, so attempts to engage their interests must be wider than with NGOs, as shown in Fig. 2.1. Conversely, NGO participants directly associated their institutional roles with practical action, as shown in Fig. 2.2. In contrast to the institutional roles of GOs in engaging, NGO respondents focused on their obligations to beneficiaries, such as timely information, responsibility of engaging, accountability and commitment.

NGOs tend to focus their responsibilities on realising specific approaches that must be considered to engage beneficiaries. In this sense, NGO participants have singularly focused on perceptions that typically involve multiple approaches to formal engagement. Unlike GOs, who lump a whole spectrum of citizens under the category of "beneficiary," NGO participants have identified specific communities or groups of people as beneficiaries for whom they work in the development context. Appendix B presents the raw data that detail the approaches GOs and NGOs associate with engaging beneficiaries. The development context in which beneficiaries reside creates the scope of BE needed for managing the development interventions. BE requires outreach to and interactions with beneficiaries to empower them and build their capacity and enable their participation. The understanding of the terminologies shapes up approaches to BE within the development activities of GOs and NGOs.

Fig. 2.2. NGOs' responses to BE

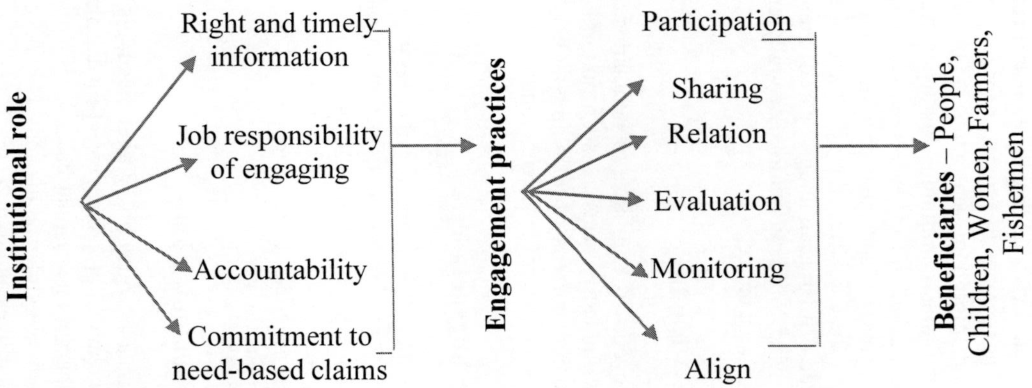

Source: based on Dutta (2021a)

BE from the Practitioners' Point of View

From development practitioners' (project personnel working in the public-sector projects, NGO fieldworkers, project personnel) point of view, engaging beneficiaries is subject to visibility, communication and capacity that development projects ensure at the field level. Here, BE demands partnership with beneficiaries to ensure social mobilisation as it is the basis for community participation. Engagement in project management means reaching target beneficiaries and informing them about development and projects. Project-management staff must communicate with beneficiaries on a regular basis, and this takes place within the government or NGO project settings. Responsible for implementation, coordination with the government and donors, and interaction with beneficiaries, the government and NGO project-management staff agreed that BE is an integral part of their roles to ensure participation. The following four key factors essentially embodied their understanding of effective engagement.

Visibility

Project staff host different events to mobilise beneficiaries. This is especially important for donor-funded projects, as such donors generally prefer visibility. Here, engagement demands partnership with beneficiaries to ensure social mobilisation and community participation.

Engaging

This forms the basis for participation. It is believed that engaging in project management leads to enhancing beneficiary participation to raise their voice. Engaging creates the scope for individuals to question the use of funds and ensure their participation in decision-making processes. In this sense, "engagement" reimagines beneficiaries as customers or clients within government or NGO development activities.

Communication

BE in project management means contacting target beneficiaries and informing them about development and projects. Project-management staff must communicate with beneficiaries on a regular basis. Communication is essential as beneficiaries need to understand what the development interventions are bringing to their lives and livelihoods.

Capacity

Projects provide training, raise awareness on the importance of developing skills and knowledge, and (from a project-management perspective), view engagement as an opportunity to develop beneficiaries. This requires the capacity of organisations in terms of both staff and finance to engage beneficiaries.

Being Engaged: As Expressed by Beneficiaries

It is interesting to see what beneficiaries think about their engagement in the development activities. The key element of BE from their point of view is to establish direct contact with GOs, NGOs or project staff to address problems, seek services, receive training and develop entrepreneurship for income generation. Thus, the following three key factors embodied their understanding.

Ability to communicate

Beneficiaries want to have access to institutions that deliver services according to their expectations. They feel confident if they can reach out to staff, for example the local Livestock Officer, who can advise them on maintaining the livestock they own. Apart from face-to-face communication, the mobile-phone network is instrumental for contacting GO or NGO fieldworkers. All beneficiaries interviewed in FGDs own a mobile phone and can access a mobile network in rural Bangladesh. They are connected to institutions and can call project staff, NGO officials or field-level government project staff directly to discuss any matters on which they seek advice.

Ability to access assistance

Field officials, such as staff in government departments, NGO fieldworkers and project staff, reside in the same localities as beneficiaries, enabling them to visit people at their homes, discuss problems and provide technical advice. According to the data, if beneficiaries request a visit to their cultivated lands or livestock or dairy farms by mobile phone, GO or NGO staff go to their households to help. As such, beneficiaries generally perceive that they are connected to the development interventions in their areas.

Next of kin

Through daily visits and regular interaction, NGO fieldworkers and GO–NGO project staff develop somewhat long-term relationships with beneficiaries. In many cases, locals will perceive certain staff like family, thus creating a comfort zone in which both groups can interact. It happens on many occasions that beneficiaries remember and contact the agricultural officer for advice even when they have been transferred to another district.

All these varied understandings that GOs, NGOs, development practitioners and beneficiaries hold lead to BE practises at the field level in the country's development context.

Engaging Beneficiaries in the Public Sector

The historical context of Bangladesh has been scrutinised in development literature to relate the country's people-oriented approach to development. Formerly part of British India (1757–1947) while belonging to the eastern region of Bengal, Bangladesh has colonial legacies (Jahan 2006) that have had a long-term effect on its economic development and democratisation. The literature expounds that the country's public sector is particularly subject to historical influence, and further notes that states with colonial pasts are more likely to inherit foreign domination in the present; indeed, this plays an instrumental role in shaping modern development (Lange 2004, 905). For Bangladesh, the end of British rule did not bring independence. Rather, the nation became part of East Pakistan because of Partition in 1947. Jahan (2006) describes this transition as Pakistani rulers replacing the British, after which the country remained under Pakistani administration from 1947 before gaining independence on December 16, 1971. It remains critical to understand how these two colonial legacies have prevailed in Bangladesh to gauge present-day attitudes on governmental approaches to development that demand integrating people at the national and local levels. The literature on administrative culture in Bangladesh strongly supports the view that colonialism in the region had significant effects on administration, national approaches to development and the government's attitude towards people who are beneficiaries of development (Hakim 1987; Jahan 2006; Jamil 2002; Zafarullah 1987; 2007; Zafarullah and Huque 2001). The relationship between the government and people is governed by bureaucracy, as the literature reveals.

Research on development assistance in Bangladesh is deeply rooted in the country's political development since 1971 and the different phases of its political history in the following decades. The literature on national development tends to examine the country's political background and development assistance in relation to its efforts to secure economic growth and policy reform. Both political instability and natural disasters remain at the centre of development discussions, where different phases of political and social change prompt different dimensions and extents of foreign assistance (Kochanek 1997; Rahman 1990; Sobhan 1979). As a relatively new democracy affected by war and environmental devastation (such as famine in 1974), Bangladesh has had to depend on external aid to implement most of its development programs since the 1970s (Raihan 2012, 240).

Bangladesh emerged as an independent country in a period when development concepts and assistance were significantly manifested by policy shifts from industrialisation to poverty reduction at the international level. Two significant development initiatives during that time include the United Kingdom's 1975 White Paper "More Aid for the Poorest" and the US International Development and Food Assistance Act of 1975 (Moyo 2009, 16). These proposals at the international level held critical importance for Bangladesh following the effects of war in 1971 and famine in 1974. As Sobhan (1979) notes, the nation had to depend on food aid during that time, but not without international interference and the demerits of dependence. Here, Bangladesh provides an example of how aid conditions can affect state policies immediately after securing national independence. Sobhan (1979, 1973) notes that food aid was instrumental in creating political sanctions in Bangladesh, pressuring the government to change its policies on food distribution and farm subsidies. Aid became a political weapon for Bangladesh when the country enforced "socialist development" against capitalism, limited privatisation and introduced a one-party system to democracy following the constitutional amendments in 1975 (Hakim and Huque 1995; Maniruzzaman 1976).

Despite changing its political system following a fifteen-year military rule, poverty alleviation in Bangladesh has persisted (Jahan 2006). It has been the popular slogan of all successive political leaderships, and has provided consistent grounds upon which the nation receives external development aid (Sobhan 1998). However, influence from discourse at an international level has since shifted the focus from poverty reduction to reform. In addition, heightened economic stability and privatisation in the 1980s affected the development process. Throughout the decade, development was significantly influenced by the WB's structural-adjustment programs (Raihan 2008; Sobhan 1998). Subsequent scrutiny of development assistance following the devastating floods in 1988 encouraged international communities to examine the ways in which aid was provided to the country.

Since then, development agencies have remained critical of aid management in Bangladesh, including its use for political purposes (Rahman 1990, 155).

Though the government administration is called centralised bureaucracy, both primary and secondary sources of data obtained for this study established that national-development planning and policies are typically grounded on two strategies: (1) commitment to development agendas at the international level, and (2) stakeholder (NGOs, private organisations, donors, think tanks, research institutes, academia, relevant ministries and departments) consultation and advocacy campaigns at the national level. However, the data also demonstrate that simply having policies is not the only criterion on which to carry out development activities; it also requires implementation at the field level to connect beneficiaries for development participation.

The scope of BE originated from the mandate of the state, which is outlined in the Constitution of the People's Republic of Bangladesh (GOB 1972). It is important to note that the Constitution was enacted in 1972 when development concepts experienced trends of community development to meet basic human needs and undertake integrated rural development.[11] These aspects of development and meeting basic needs are reflected in the Constitution. For example, Article 7 recognises people as being the "source of all powers of the Republic," while Part II outlines the "Fundamental Principles of State Policy." Several articles in this section are directly related to people's right to participate in development and democratic processes. Article 21 defines the responsibilities of rights holders (citizens) and service providers (public service). In line with the duty of citizens to abide by the Constitution and the law, it is the duty of public servants "to strive at all times to serve the people" (Article 21, Section 2). The key principle is that people are at the centre of all development activities assumed by the nation that has just obtained independence. Therefore, development planning is inclusive of people; not an isolated national priority but integrated into the government-policy apparatus. Government ministries and departments are responsible for the design, planning and implementation of projects in consultation with various stakeholders, which creates scope for BE. For example, development programs in health, agriculture and disaster management allow BE through collecting data from the field level, engaging farmers through the demonstration of technology and crop productions, and disaster preparedness programs for local communities and volunteers.

---

[11] The development approach during the early 1970s, as mentioned in Leal (2007, 540). The Constitution of the People's Republic of Bangladesh was formed in 1972, following independence.

However, it is also evident that BE is based on addressing the needs of locals. This implies that the beneficiary requirements are assessed by the relevant authority at the field level, which in turn forms the basis for the government's development planning. The scope of this strategy to give beneficiaries a "say" in development planning, as Lukensmeyer and Torres (2006) define it, or create scope for their roles in decision making, as Eversole (2010) argues, cannot be denied. Though, instead of demonstrating "dissatisfaction" with the current policy or making demands on the state that Roberts (2004) and Gaventa (2002) consider for engagement, conveying the needs is how people are engaged in the public-sector context of Bangladesh. Whether BE results in participation or "voluntary dedication" (Krull 1999) is another area that requires attention in the country's development context.

Long-term development planning and different service-sector policies under which individual ministries and departments operate include BE. The FYPs articulated the need to ensure people's participation in the country's development. From this point of view, development planning in Bangladesh seems to be documented as people-focused, aligns with people-oriented development concepts, and is reflected in the identification of development issues. The first FYP[12] in 1973 asserted the need for political commitment and the ability to mobilise people for nation building (GOB 1972). Recognising the young generation's contribution to the independence of the country, the first FYP encouraged leadership and organisations to "mobilize their talent and energies towards productive ends" (GOB 1972, 5). The fourth FYP outlined development strategies for the rural population through appropriate organisational and institutional mechanisms for participatory planning, including women's participation (GOB 1995), along with different service-sector development strategies. The fifth FYP (GOB n. d.) added a new dimension to development planning, which shifted from central planning to participatory planning by strengthening local-government institutions (LGIs), introducing local-level participatory planning and integrating local-level development projects into national-development planning.[13] The sixth FYP[14] considered the effective participation of poor people and women in anti-poverty programs to be an indicator of development achievements. Similarly, the seventh FYP (GOB 2016) related community participation to these areas and prioritised addressing broad-based participation in achieving inclusive and sustainable growth. These are some of the significant shifts in the government that, on one hand, have a long history of colonisation and which invite criticism through disconnecting

[12] Section 1.5 of the first FYP formulated after independence.
[13] Chapter II, Section 2.2.4, in the fifth FYP.
[14] Chapter 1, in the sixth FYP (GOB 2012).

with people, and on the other make the development planning pro-people that GOs need to implement at the field level.

NGOs and BE

NGOs operate within the institutional and legal framework of the Bangladesh Government and their functions are guided by the constitutional provisions and laws of the state. While operating within the government's institutional and legal frameworks, data from interviews demonstrated that the inclusion of BE in NGO policies is based on two concepts: it is subject to the implementation of government policies, and it was NGO advocacy and campaigns on human-development issues, inclusion and participation that led to the formulation of government policies. Tarannum (2009) provides a chronology of strategies spanning four generations of NGO work in Bangladesh, from 1971 (immediately following independence) to date. While the first generation of organisations intended to meet the immediate needs of a war-torn population, the second focused more on "micro-interventions" for community development. Now receiving foreign funds, the third iteration of NGOs in the 1980s contributed significantly to rural development in line with a global movement towards greater local-level participation in development. Currently, fourth-generation groups seek "changes in specific policies and institutions" (Tarannum 2009, 30–3), reflecting more global aspects of policy advocacy. Given the number and scope of NGO-led activities in socio-economic development, it is safe to say that Bangladesh is a hub for NGO growth.[15]

The development literature critically analyses the NGOs in Bangladesh as an institutional base to minimise gaps in the public sector and address political crises while under military rule until the 1990s. Haque (2002) mentions that NGO expansion was not affected during this period of non-democratic control from 1975 to 1990. In fact, the number of nongovernment agents (both local and foreign) increased from 101 in 1975 to 461 by 1990–1 (Bangladesh Financial Intelligence Unit 2015). Within the same context, Batley (2011, 308) mentions that changes in the national power structure and its military regime did not affect the role of NGOs.[16] Rather, the presence of donors enabled their survival and empowered them to continue their functions under different political controls. Furter, as Haque (2002,

[15] NGOAB has more than 2,200 active NGOs (including international NGOs) listed (NGOAB 2022).

[16] There were two military coups in 1975 and 1982. Martial law continued for a long time alongside forming political parties and electing leading generals as the presidents of the country.

414) notes, the military control between 1982 and 1990 saw the significant growth of NGOs due to "the regime's efforts to enhance its legitimacy at the grassroots level" and "use large NGOs as substitutes for opposition political parties." Besides political, social and economic factors, NGO growth was further attributed to "over population, rural poverty and landlessness" (Haque 2002, 414).

While NGO policies do not contradict national-development planning, interviews reveal that a participatory approach to development is in practice in the NGO sector, which has led to the conceptualisation of BE in government policies. This is evident in the case of women's empowerment, bringing women out of traditional household work to non-traditional activities, such as using motorbikes for fieldwork, driving, farming and entrepreneurship. A critical finding from interviews with a respondent from the Department of Women Affairs (DWA) revealed that NGO contributions to women's mobilisation are important: it is the NGOs that first started giving women bicycles to get to work in the field level. It was possible to engage women, as is seen today due to NGO campaigns, and this was a significant development. NGO objectives on BE (shown in Box 1) focus on specific areas of work because different NGOs work on different issues, which result in different projects with "people" as a core value.

The organisational objectives of NGOs cover people, poverty and disadvantaged and vulnerable groups of people. Including "people" means creating opportunities for poor and disadvantaged communities, including women in rural areas, to work as a catalyst for poverty alleviation and social and economic development. As NGO policies are expected not to contradict the core development agenda of the government, they carry out services to target populations. Government policies form the basis of development initiatives for NGOs, and as such, being governed by rules and regulations does not necessarily create limitations for NGOs in engaging beneficiaries. Instead, participatory provisions in government policies create opportunities for NGOs to ensure BE, as revealed during interviews with government and NGO respondents.

In 2013, the GOB officially recognised nongovernment contributions to development in its nationwide consultations with NGOs. The GOB considers its strategic relationship with nongovernment sectors as a collaborative endeavour through which it facilitates partnership in development activities. In particular, NGO contributions towards achieving the MDGs and implementation of development projects are well documented in the NGOAB's (2013, 15–20) report on consultations. As noted, while the government remains chiefly responsible for policy formulation, NGOs work as collaborative partners in terms of policy advocacy and project implementation under administrative rule. NGO attempts to mobilise foreign

Box 1. Beneficiary integration into NGO objectives

BRAC: We act as a catalyst, creating opportunities for **people** living in poverty to realise their potential.

ASA: The institutional mission of ASA is to support and strengthen the economy **at the bottom** of the socio-economic pyramid by facilitating access to financial services for the **poor, marginalised and disadvantaged**.

Grameen Bank: Ensure that the credit system serves **the poor** and not vice versa. Credit officers visit villages, enabling them to get to know the borrowers (one of the Methods of Action).

Grameen Australia: Grameen Australia is leading the way in the development of social businesses to provide employment for **the poor** and the skills and financial responsibility to permanently escape poverty.

Madaripur Legal Aid Association (MLAA): Access to justice increased for the empowerment of **disadvantaged people**, particularly women and children.

Environment and Social Development Organization (ESDO): Reduction in the income poverty and human poverty of the **people** in the working area through undertaking massive integrated development programs for the **poor** and **marginalised communities** through service delivery and a rights-based approach.

BASTOB: Envisioning a society in which **poor and disadvantaged people** are socially developed and economically self-reliant.

Sources: websites of these NGOs accessed 2015–9

resources are particularly noteworthy within the development context of Bangladesh. Here, the government claims it makes such efforts possible through accommodating development policies and by providing ongoing support. It is important to note (in accordance with primary data) that receiving foreign resources for NGO-implemented projects creates the scope for aligning BE strategies in project management with donor policies.

Note here that the Palli Karma-Sahayak Foundation (PKSF) was established by the government in 1990. As a development organisation that works for "sustainable poverty reduction through income generation," it operates, through its core programs and projects, by providing financial resources as loans or grants to its partner organisations (NGOs) for project implementation (PKSF n. d.).

GOs, NGOs and Beneficiaries: The Relational Dynamics

The general perception of GOs in Bangladesh usually conjures associations with a top-down administration exercising control and authority over nongovernment sectors. Indeed, the government has formal power over these entities in the form of regulatory and institutional rule. Various legislations on NGOs and foreign donations regulate NGO functions in Bangladesh, and the NGO Affairs Bureau (NGOAB) is the formal organisation that monitors NGO functions and foreign aid flowing to NGOs (Haque 2002, 418).

Broadly speaking, the literature condemns the power structure underlying GO–NGO relations, citing the former's control over the latter and the attitudes of public-sector officials towards both NGO executives and staff as particularly oppressive (Ahmad 2002; Jamil 1998; Karim 1996; Sanyal 1991). Generally, GOs exert more control over NGOs when they feel threatened by NGO influence on, for example, mobilising people against the government or participating in political activities encouraging policy change (Hashemi 1996). Power also derives from NGOs' ability to manipulate donors into diverting funds from government projects, closing income gaps and threatening difference through the alternative lifestyle observations of NGO leaders (Haque 2002, 419; Hashemi 1996; Sanyal 1991, 1370). Here, Karim (1996, 137) points out that members of the government and political parties in Bangladesh generally view NGOs negatively. The most common criticisms held include the overlap of roles, lack of coordination and high administrative costs involved in their running. Similarly, NGO observations on government, according to Sanyal (1991, 1371), cite the "us vs them" divide between each sphere as the main source of disparity. In the past, donors' perceived scepticism about government efficiency led to added support for NGOs in many Asian and sub-Saharan countries, causing "resentment and hostility" in the public sector (Jamil 1998, 43). Ahmad's (2002, 101) research notes similar findings, citing examples in which government officials openly opposed the popularity and influence of NGOs, as they are supposedly used to enjoying "immense power at the local and national levels in Bangladesh." That said, research on local NGOs seems particularly critical about their accountability towards beneficiaries. Karim (1996, 139) describes NGO duties by highlighting how these organisations are regularly accountable to their respective Board of Governors or Executive Committee. Ahmed and Rafi (1999, 6) note that it is social mobilisation (for which people turn to nongovernment forces) that makes these bodies "acceptable to the people and earn their credibility by offering programs in which people have confidence and become gainer by associating with them."

Limitations also exist at the NGO level in progressing the development results. Worse, evidence shows that NGOs do not incorporate the opinions of beneficiaries in their decision making (Tarannum 2009, 14, 80), while forging the dependency of the poor and charging higher interest on microcredit allowances. This leads to the biased selection of less advantaged social groups needing loans, as well as the limited capacity of the underprivileged to bargain with NGOs (Islam 2016, 1186–7). The lack of accountability towards service recipients is a governance issue further identified in one qualitative study by Transparency International Bangladesh (TIB) (2007), combining desk research with fieldwork and fact finding on twenty NGOs in Bangladesh. The TIB report said that NGO reports exaggerate the service recipients, which is a key problem concerning NGO accountability towards beneficiaries.

BE and Development Assistance

While identifying the scope of GO–NGO policies to engage development beneficiaries, donor conditions have been revealed as one of the major factors for BE in the development context of Bangladesh. It is indubitable that donors will influence aid-recipient countries and guide development strategies. Integrating people is the one certain outcome of donor conditions as the gradual progression of development (see Table 1.2) at the international level channels local contexts through development assistance. The development literature talks about donor conditions and how these affect the purpose, attention and practises of people-oriented development within global and local contexts, where the concept resides within the determinants of "good" and "bad." The literature seems to take a justifying approach to development assistance and argues that underdeveloped countries cannot progress without external assistance (Smith 1986, 29); it also cannot be said that foreign aid in this context is "unimportant" (Caporaso 1980, 607). Added to this, Coomaraswamy (2012) analysed the importance of foreign assistance in relation to closing the gap between beneficiary countries and donors, changes in donor–recipient country relationships, and the need to identify why and when aid affects development. Generally, the bad part of it implies that help is ineffective, and vice versa. Alesina and Dollar (2000, 37) explain how aid is strategically related to the conditions of recipient countries. Debate on the purpose of developmental aid includes the political and strategic interests of donor countries despite intentions to provide crisis support, reduce poverty and preserve human rights in recipient nations (Riddell 2007).

Despite its influence in development discussions, the context in which people are expected to be integrated is critical for the organisations responsible for providing aid at the local level (e.g. aid agencies, GOs and NGOs), which need to address the requirements of engaging people in the development process. Thus far, the discourse provides no clear answer regarding whether BE has been instrumental in sustaining development success. The discussion has also created the scope to examine whether donor influence or development assistance creates a space for public involvement relative to different national contexts. As Sen (1999) emphasises, development goals are primarily designed for people, and understanding these goals should create a space for their participation in development. Indeed, there is an equal need to examine the roles of organisations, but above all an urgency to acknowledge public perceptions on improvement and how individuals' own understandings are being facilitated in that process of development participation.

Bangladesh receives foreign funding for different development sectors. Rather than depending solely on foreign aid, Bangladesh continued to restructure its economy while addressing the emergent trends in foreign aid, which favoured governance reform. This approach to development and administrative efficiency that the country adopted aligned with the foreign-aid agenda of the 1990s, addressing both governance and community participation of the nation's people as promoted by the DAC and OECD (Führer 1996). It is also related to the World Bank's aid provision, which afforded money specifically for governance reform and sustainable economic growth (Moyo 2009, 22–3). For Bangladesh, this trend of restructuring, governance and development implies less dependence on aid and more focus on foreign investment, trade, export and remittance to upscale the growth it gradually experienced throughout the 1990s and 2000s, as identified by Raihan (2012). Further, both FDIs and policy reform were responsible for enhancing the country's steady economic growth (Tabassum and Ahmed 2014). Here, Amin and Murshed (2017, 104) consider four categories of foreign inflow – aid, FDIs, investment and remittance – that were instrumental for the significant performance in the "attainment of sustainable economic development" in Bangladesh.

National-development planning newly focused on achieving both the MDGs and SDGs with greater emphasis on sustainable human development in health, population, education, technology and ICT (Raihan 2012).

However, focusing on "good" governance and orientation to people in development does not necessarily mean that external assistance has ceased in Bangladesh. Rather, aid contributes to its continued economic growth and development, which are spheres that are very distinct by definition, as they relate to the concept of human development. Here, Kosack and Tobin (2006, 208) argue that aid supports economic expansion by increasing the nation's workforce capacity; however, economic growth likewise contributes to further investment in human development itself. This concept relates to trends in foreign aid to Bangladesh, as more help comes in the form of project assistance and ADP funding (Raihan 2012, 257). This is particularly evident in an ERD (n. d.) report that shows a decline in food aid from 1,102 metric tons between 1972 and 1973 to 87.6 metric tons between 2015 and 2016. In contrast, project aid increased from 68.08 million to 85.88 million within the same period. Given this, restructuring economic growth and changes in support purposes do not necessarily negate the country's focus on connecting people to development. Naturally, development assistance provided to Bangladesh reflects donor preferences for the inclusion of people and influences the government's development planning to incorporate this provision (in the form of participation) in policies. Whether it is donor conditions for development assistance or commitment to development treatises and declarations, the government considers BE in pursuit of its development participation, as revealed during fieldwork. It is said that development-funding provisions include the BE element, and this is very important for donors as it creates the scope for GOs to include BE in its development agenda. From the development partner's point of view, engaging project beneficiaries forms the basis for considering any development assistance program for Bangladesh. Funding development programs have a major focus on BE to monitor the extent to which the assistance is reaching its target beneficiaries, specifically the marginalised and vulnerable groups, and therefore social inclusion matters.

Similarly, NGO-led development interventions involve beneficiaries because most of these are donor funded and also have conditions. Being considered an "action group" of change, these organisations became agents of development in Bangladesh, mainly because of donor advocacy and partnership (Islam and Walkerden 2015; Haider 2011; Rahman 2006; Sarker 2005). In their efforts, NGOs are seemingly capable of mobilising the poor and organising their participation in rural development through grassroots alignment and disaster-resilience capacity. Accordingly, Sarker

Fig. 2.3. Integration of BE and monitoring in donor-funded projects

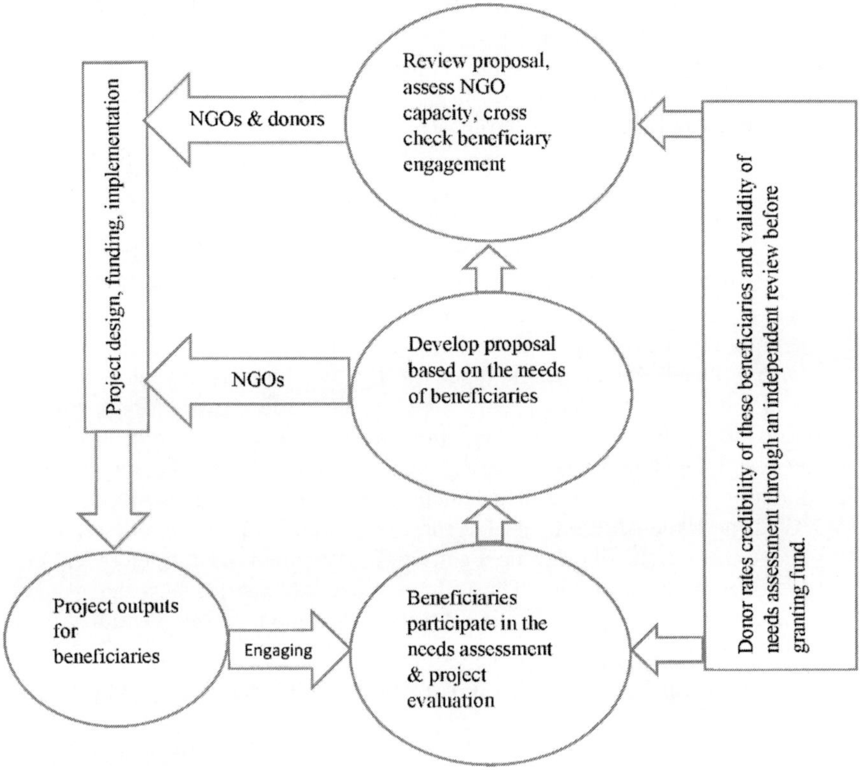

Source: Dutta (2021a)

(2005) viewed their role in relation to the concept of NPM, arguing that, in comparison to GOs, NGOs demonstrate success in providing certain basic services through creative and situational approaches. NGOs link rural people to markets and entrepreneurial activities, offer autonomous-management strategies and group mobilisation, and invest in human-resources development (Sarker 2005). While donor influence is a conditioning factor in government policies and development programs, it is equally applicable for NGOs while implementing the government's development programs or donor-funded programs. It is more obvious for NGOs as they receive donor funds that come with agenda-based funding and have their own priority. Given the preference of donors for BE, NGOs admit that donors take engagement seriously and monitor whether NGOs' connections with target populations exist, as shown in Fig. 2.3.

In Bangladesh, BE is not simply a matter of contracts and templates for NGOs, but also involves physical monitoring by donor agencies. The diagram in Fig. 2.3 was provided by an NGO executive, and demonstrates how practical development interventions, coordination and monitoring could occur at the field level for BE undertaken by NGOs receiving and implementing foreign-aided projects.

Transferring Policies into Practises

Given the scope of BE in the public and NGO sectors, there are several key factors that transfer policies into practises enabling GOs and NGOs to engage beneficiaries for development participation. While development planning narrates social inclusion in the public sector, individual service-sector policies appear to be open to BE, which was revealed during interviews with different groups of research participants. For example, provisions of beneficiary participation in relevant service-sector policies, rules and legislation have created the basis for BE in the day-to-day functions of government departments across service sectors and UPs. NGOs, with their presence at the rural level, reach out to beneficiaries to engage them in the development activities they undertake, funded by either the government or donors. The following sections narrate how and when beneficiaries are engaged within GO–NGO development interventions.

Engaging beneficiaries within GO–NGO project contexts

Development projects are the institutional basis for the management of development assistance, implementation of development programs and the involvement of beneficiaries in the implementation of project components. They have always implemented development initiatives in either the government or NGO sectors (Eversole 2010). Projects deliver the intended services to target populations with either GOs or NGOs as development assistance, funded locally or from international aid, entailing the purpose of responding to local needs through a management structure (Abraham 2014; Führer 1996). International-development assistance consists of projects for which funds are channelled to interventions in different service sectors, tourism and cultural projects, and trade, and the recent trends include democracy, human rights and peace projects (Riddell 2007, 180). Projects with international-development assistance also cover development-project settings in the public sector, such as "infrastructure, utilities, agriculture, transportation, water, electricity, energy, sewage, mines, health, nutrition, population and urban development, education, environment, social development, reform and governance" (Ika and Donnelly 2017, 45). Development projects[17] are the main tools for GOs and NGOs to transfer policies into practises in carrying out development participation through BE. It was noted during interviews that BE occurs within GO–NGO project settings when it has a specific requirement. For example, BE occurs if required by donors, or stated in the project document or in a project context where NGOs need to disburse microcredits.

As with GOs, the BE component of projects is convenient for NGOs because they connect beneficiaries through small projects, as was mentioned by an NGO respondent. Furthermore, an interview with an NGO executive revealed that BE is a project component. Apart from projects, individual NGO strategies were also instrumental to engaging project beneficiaries, as were NGOs' own long-term (five-year) strategic plans that include a BE strategy. For NGOs, BE is related to project planning for funding or the implementation of donor or government-funded projects. Development projects are related to BE (see Appendix C) in terms of management, personnel, NGO implementation, project templates, service delivery and donors. Both GOs and NGOs find BE convenient when it is integrated into development projects. Beneficiaries are connected to projects through capacity development, income generation or receiving microcredits for undertaking income-generation activities. BE has been considered a project component and is evident mainly in the project-implementation phase. Whatever strategies are in place to transfer policies into practises, development projects are the basis for BE. GOs and NGOs consider projects and project components critical for BE, and there is no contradiction between GO and NGO perceptions on this finding.

Local administration: NGOs and BE

Implementing public-sector development projects at the local level, allowing local people to participate, is the major concept argued in favour of decentralisation (Devas and Grant 2003; Bardhan 2002; Mohan and Stokke 2000; Conyers 1984). It is important for GOs to ensure service provisions within reach of communities. The decentralised structure of service providers is inevitable in creating service provisions for communities and engaging beneficiaries at the local level. The critical factors for BE appeared to be largely related to the decentralisation of services at the field level. Research participants categorised the provision of decentralised services into two groups: in local administration and in UPs.

---

[17] As mentioned in chapter one and shown in Appendix A.

GOs are responsible for the management of development programs at the field level, which are mainly implemented through various government departments and local administrations under relevant line ministries. Government-service sectors like agriculture, health and education, social services and women's development are decentralised to the field level. Each UPZ has headquarters under different line ministries, which is extended to the union level in the service sector. For example, the Department of Agricultural Extension (DAE) remains responsible for implementing agricultural development projects at the district, UPZ and union levels. Down to the rural level, each union has three sub-assistant agriculture officers who work closely with farmers. Interviews with district, UPZ and union-agriculture officials demonstrated that, given the service-providing nature of the DAE, it needs to work directly with farmers, who are the primary beneficiaries. The central focus of the DAE is to have its planning, implementation, monitoring and evaluation in close connection with its stakeholders, including farmers, NGOs and government agencies at the field level under agricultural-extension projects.

Similarly, the Directorate of Health and UPZ Health Complex is a vast and complex area of health services that covers the community, maternal health, nutrition and many other health related development activities from district to union levels. At the field level, the health administration is responsible for the management of district hospitals, UPZ health complexes, union sub-centres and community clinics. Program guidelines are sent from the directorate to the field-level offices, where union health and family-planning officers (UH&FPO) are responsible for the implementation of the government's health programs at the district, UPZ and union levels. Family-welfare volunteers (FWVs) are present at the union level to reach individual households and directly interact with beneficiaries. The community-healthcare provider (CHCP) supplies first aid in the community clinics, and there are female staff who provide support in skilled births. Currently, there are fourteen thousand community clinics in operation that encourage the development organisations to provide support to the implementation community clinic (WHO n. d.). The CHCP project data demonstrates that there was a 48% increase of beneficiaries seeking community-clinic services between 2011 and 2013 (Nargis n. d.). The Totthoapa project,[18] under the Ministry of Women and Children Affairs (MoWCA), provides information services to rural women. Instead of having M&E offices at the field level, the project runs e-monitoring that requires reporting on

[18] "Tottho" is a Bengali word meaning "information," and "apa" represents the elder sister in the cultural context of Bangladesh.

courtyard meetings, door-to-door service provisions and beneficiary data (MoWCA 2022) at the union level.

Despite the administrative network of GOs at the field level, research participants held strong views about NGO networks within communities at the grassroots level, which they believe are helpful for these organisations to engage the project beneficiaries. NGOs can go door-to-door and are more intimate with beneficiaries than government officials, as was mentioned by a government official. The presence of NGOs at the grassroots level enables these organisations to engage beneficiaries. They are based at the district and UPZ levels and have strong networks within communities at the union level. Travelling to households from district to UPZ or from UPZ to union is an everyday activity for NGO fieldworkers. These door-to-door visits are criteria for success in NGO engaging communities. For example, family-planning projects using this approach were successful, as a government official revealed during an interview. Primary-data sources reveal that strategies of having administrative networks at the field level were essential for GOs and NGOs to engage beneficiaries. The presence of NGOs at the grassroots level is well recognised by GO and NGO respondents; however, the administrative network of GOs is an additional support for NGOs to engage beneficiaries (see chapter five), as revealed during interviews.

Engaging in UPs

Policy provisions empower local-government institutions (LGIs), such as UPs in Bangladesh, to engage rural people in the process of local development. Government policies in Bangladesh also make UPs responsible for BE, which was reflected in the Union Parishad Act 2009. The Union Parishad (Development Planning) Rules 2013 connected beneficiaries through ward committees directly to the government's development programs, which specify strategies for including beneficiaries to identify project needs, existing challenges and economic opportunities. The Union Parishad Act 2009 creates the scope for BE at the grassroots level. Its rules clearly state engagement strategies used by local-government institutes. UP gets block grants and the selection criteria include an open-budget system that directly engages beneficiaries through participatory budgeting, as shown in Fig. 2.4. The act and its implementation rules allow UPs to engage communities through ward committees in the local-development process.

Fig. 2.4. Community engagement in local development

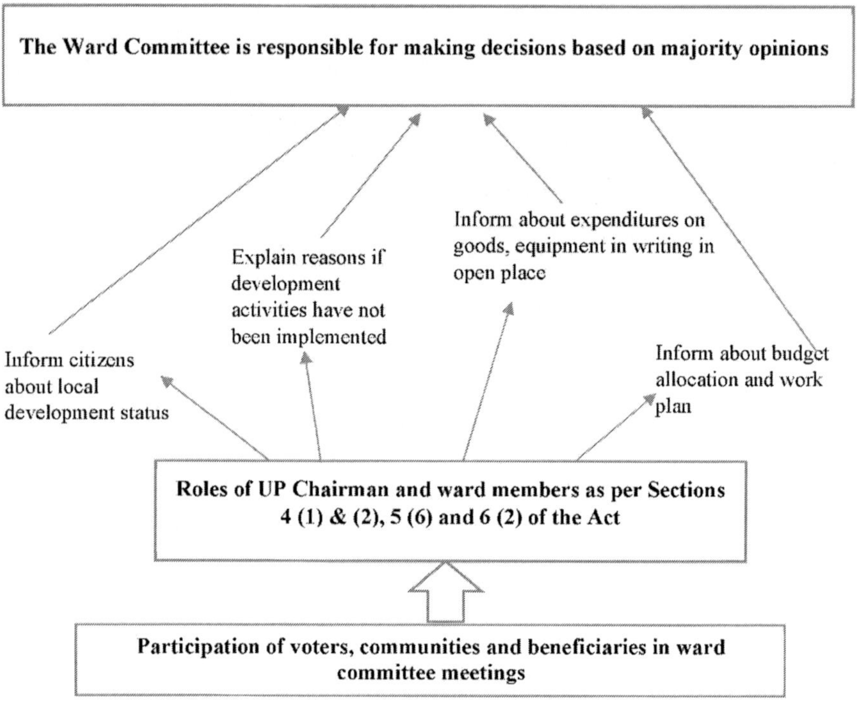

Source: Dutta (2021a)

Devas and Grant (2003, 308) observed that the traditional model of LGIs, in which citizens had no role between elections and the elected representatives make decisions on behalf of citizens, prevails in many countries. However, the above provisions, as stated in the UP Act 2009, reject this traditional role and create the scope for BE to achieve development participation. In this process of integration, UP accountability is expected to provide local populations with opportunities to participate in the development activities undertaken by the government. The notion of participation is a dimension of decentralisation, which can produce a "multiplicity of local developments which are determined by the local people themselves" (Mohan and Stokke 2000, 252). Research participants thought that this decentralisation of development activities significantly contributes to BE at the lowest tier of administrative units in Bangladesh and is supportive of development participation at the grassroots level.

NGOs considered the involvement of UPs to be critical for BE. It was the local people who were expected to provide feedback on the project context and the need for improvement. UPs can play an important role while local people need to be engaged and contribute to planning, monitoring and evaluating development interventions. In many cases, NGOs seek support from the UP chairperson and representatives to communicate project benefits to the people, as revealed in interviews with NGOs. This is because rural communities are more familiar with UP representatives than NGO staff. UP's involvement in beneficiary engagement is supportive of NGOs' activities because, in the absence of this institution, decisions may be referred to a higher level, which can cause delays and less appropriate outcomes (see Uphoff 2014) for NGOs.

Guidelines for engaging beneficiaries

For GOs, it is the implementation guidelines to engage beneficiaries that individual departments receive from line ministries that they need to follow. Research participants revealed that, in following the guidelines, the scope of development planning and policies at the national level creates provisions for BE at the field level. For example, engaging beneficiaries is outlined in the diary of the sub-assistant agriculture officer, who oversees a union-agriculture office and is responsible for door-to-door visits at the field level, enabling farmers to directly receive services from the DAE. The diary outlines the everyday tasks of the official, including how to assist farmers in the identification of problems and remedies, planning of agricultural block extension based on individual needs, gathering agriculture information and linking farmers to other relevant offices for assistance on agricultural activities. Similarly, FWVs provide family-planning support services at the union level following the UP Health and Family Planning Centre Management Guidelines, which provide the necessary information and skills on how to engage beneficiaries. Policies at the national level provide guidelines that make the staff–beneficiary interaction mandatory and contact target beneficiaries regularly, as identified by the research participants.

NGOs usually follow different methods to engage beneficiaries, and NGO workers are skilled in using different tools for this. Household surveys, courtyard meetings, beneficiary group meetings, trainings, advocacy, microcredit management and interactions with beneficiaries are some of the engagement tools that NGO workers utilise. NGOs are guided by the principles of the Human Rights Based Approach (HRBA), Women in Development (WID), Community Action Plan, Early Childcare Development, Project Management and Sustainable Development, Participatory Reflection and mapping of Social Wellbeing. Following government guidelines also occurs for NGOs implementing development programs. For example, partner NGOs that obtained funds from PKSF need to follow its guidelines for project planning, implementation and community engagement (PKSF n. d.).

Technical expertise and staff presence at the local level

While interviewees perceived decentralised administration as a means of engaging beneficiaries in the service sectors, the presence of staff at the field level and their technical expertise were equally critical for reaching and integrating communities in development activities, which was revealed during interviews with agriculture and health officials. The district administration claimed that the presence of government agriculture staff at the field level is very strong, which is the main reason for the miracle advancement of agriculture in Bangladesh. This appears to be slightly different in other service sectors, such as health. For example, the central level official in the Directorate of Health said that field level health officials (in the public-health sector) remain responsible for the implementation of health projects at the field level, but existing staff strength at the field level was lower than planned for in the departmental organigram. Despite having the government mandate to deliver healthcare services to rural people, a lack of staff (doctors) constricts the scope of engaging beneficiaries in this sector. At the time of interview (April 2017), only four out of twenty-two doctors were posted to one UPZ health office. In addition, due to the lack of appropriate infrastructure at the union level, medical professionals mainly stay at the UPZ or district levels, as revealed by the UH&FPO.

Shared benefits and BE

Interviews revealed that when communities are informed of development benefits in government initiatives such as food for education, educational stipends, financial benefits or benefits of local infrastructure, they are more engaged. For example, free primary education, projects like girl students' stipends, or income-generation activities for dropout girl students created a positive impact for BE in the education sector. Social inclusion has increased for programs such as the old-age allowance, vulnerable-group development (VGD) cards and allowances in which GOs create opportunities for shared benefits to target populations. Similarly, target beneficiaries are engaged in different projects under the Forestry Department, in which they receive a portion of benefits for the maintenance of forests.

In this view, providing small loans or financial support to beneficiaries appears to be critical for NGOs to engage beneficiaries. NGOs are also involved in government-development projects to implement financial-incentive components. For example, the donor-funded agricultural extension project has a microcredit component for farmers, which is implemented by an NGO. In addition, NGOs create value chains for farmers and small entrepreneurs to market agriculture production and goods, which is an example of how the community benefit from NGOs and participate in the process of engaging in NGO-implemented projects.

Capacity development and BE

NGOs and GOs engage target beneficiaries by providing training in different service sectors. As identified during interviews, the capacity-development strategy is used to transfer specific skills or technologies, to build awareness on development initiatives and to enhance entrepreneurship for income-generation activities. However, research participants revealed that government staff, like UPZ or union-agriculture officers, provide training to beneficiaries, even in NGO-implemented projects or training components arranged by NGOs. Having specialised staff like doctors or agriculture officers enables NGOs to conduct hands-on professional training and demonstrations. The government's program on youth development enhances the capacity of youths with the objective of creating a skilled workforce, as mentioned by an NGO executive. Similarly, training is provided to health workers on immunisation, safe motherhood and skilled births where public-health officials provide hands-on training to health workers, who then transfer the knowledge and skills to midwives and women in individual households.

Involving communities and volunteers

Engagement also occurs in the involvement of communities and volunteers by GOs. Interviewees identified that BE was ensured through the purposive engagement of communities and volunteers. In establishing community clinics and primary schools, UPs can engage well-off families in rural areas, who provide land and support the construction of clinics and school infrastructure in specific areas. This community support for establishing community clinics and primary schools leads to BE in development initiatives and goes beyond the traditional government policy of land acquisition and paying compensation.

Digital facilities, communication and engagement

Internet services, the mobile network and the provision of digital information portals have made BE easier, as identified by research participants. For example, information and communication technology for development (ICT4D) is a recent dimension which argues in favour of the openness of development (Loudon and Rivett 2013; Smith, Elder and Emdon 2011). The question of connecting regions without infrastructure was answered through the provision of wireless connectivity to poor communities in developing countries (Heeks 2008). During interviews, government respondents considered the internet, mobile phones and websites to be the main logistics that enable them to effectively engage communities in development programs. The use of mobile phones and network coverage plays a significant role in Bangladesh. According to the Bangladesh Telecommunication Regulatory Commission (BTRC), the number of mobile-phone subscribers was 150,945 in June 2018 (BTRC n. d.). Beneficiaries in the rural areas own mobile phones, and in some cases have smart phones as well.

From the beneficiary point of view, mobile-phone networks are instrumental for connecting to service providers in public and NGO sectors. Interviews with beneficiaries revealed that they have the mobile numbers of government and NGO officials or field workers, which enables them to contact the concerned offices at any time if there are problems. The beneficiaries of agriculture-development projects believed it was useful to receive text messages from union officials as it helped in transferring important information instantly. Digital facilities enabled beneficiaries to interact with each other and GO–NGO staff, as identified during interviews with beneficiaries.

The Union Information Service Centres (UISC) in UPs further add to BE because rural communities come to UP for information on various services and ICT training. Similarly, DAE has the Agriculture Information Service, which demonstrates relevant agricultural information for farmers and agriculture officials. Mobile applications for call centres (e.g. 16123), community radio and e-agriculture are some of the digital-communication facilities through which beneficiaries are engaged. All monthly e-agriculture magazines are available through the Agriculture Information Service portal.[19] Digital-communication facilities add value to BE and connect the central and local administrations, which speeds up decision making. Communication technologies, Wi-Fi, computers and laptops in

[19] See www.ais.gov.bd.

local administrations make it easy and quick for local staff to coordinate with central offices, as revealed during interviews.

Communicating development benefits

Although mobile phones are handy for communicating with GO and NGO officials and communities, they may not be the only means of communicating development benefits to beneficiaries. Therefore, communicating project benefits to target populations is a major task, which was identified by research participants. The UH&FPO interviewed argued that engaging beneficiaries involves directly communicating with them. For example, to achieve the government's primary-health programs, staff need to go to people with communication skills to convey messages to them, and providing treatment is not the only way to reach people as doctors traditionally do. Health and nutrition education is a primary-level need for which awareness programs are carried out under primary-healthcare programs. This is how beneficiaries should be connected to the government's health programs, the official stated.

In brief, development planning in Bangladesh is open to engagement in its provision of participation and strikes a balance between theories, concepts and local contexts. While accelerating people-focused development and the expansion of NGOs, which have covered most of the development discussions since the 1970s and 1990s, a cautious articulation is evident in relation to GO–NGO roles, institutional accountability and the responsibilities of UPs to ensure people are integrated into development. The development planning remains people centred in FYPs, as is usually argued for in the development literature. A safeguard is to make NGOs more accountable to GOs; however, these strategies also allow NGOs to work with beneficiaries in the field, as identified in the following chapters. This being said, the "people-centred" development has been a component of the development planning of GOs and is not solely an NGO agenda to ensure development participation. The government has expanded the role of UPs to ensure that local communities are involved in local-level development. In addition, the concept of ICT4D has been integrated into the political and development campaign, which research participants considered to be a tool to engage beneficiaries. However, donor influence seems to be instrumental for GOs and NGOs and creates opportunities for BE. Whatever strategies are in place to transfer policies into practises, these incubate within development projects, as discussed in the next chapter.

CHAPTER THREE

ENGAGING BENEFICIARIES FOR PARTICIPATION: HOW AND WHEN

Along with discussions on how development encompasses local contexts and organisations within the process of development participation, approaches to BE need to respond to various local factors in each individual country. In practice, the concept of development participation has advanced across projects through which development assistance is provided at both the local and international levels. Development initiatives are thus "typically" posited "within projects and programs managed and funded by professionals in organisations" (Eversole 2010, 30). Abraham (2014, 1) defines these efforts as "a series of activities that aim at solving problems within a given time frame with a clear set of objectives" for individual benefit. At the international level, development assistance is based on guided principles of project appraisal. This notion was officially adopted in 1988 to cover the entire process of project management, from initial project identification to preparation, appraisal, selection and design, and even subsequent monitoring and evaluation (Führer 1996, 50). In the development field, the key project goals mainly encompass various agenda to reduce poverty, build beneficiary capacity, provide services and capital for income generation, women's development and entrepreneurship, and upgrade the livelihood of local people. The participation of beneficiaries, the key stakeholders, is instrumental in achieving the project goals. BE is inevitable in this process to ensure their participation.

To illustrate development participation, scholars and practitioners have generated discussions on why (reasons for participation) and how (projects, methods and techniques to create scope for participation) people should participate in development. The "why" aspects advocate for its importance in obtaining the commitment and support of communities to back certain projects (Oakley and Marsden 1984, 13). Gaventa and Valderrama (1999, 2) stress the need to link citizens at local and grassroots levels, as it is considered a means of "strengthening relevance, quality and sustainability" through increased representation or accountability, superior articulation of grassroots needs and priorities, and linking development to the state. Conversely, the "how" part of engagement encompasses several strategies and approaches, which Oakley et al. (1991, 167–73) tie to project issues. The provision of these efforts, and their management, governance and implementation, seems to ground the general basis for participation. This relation between projects and participation has been outlined in various development initiatives by identifying approaches of integrating beneficiaries in development. Certain processes to document and illustrate collaboration between stakeholders, recognition of geographical differences, forming groups of beneficiaries and stakeholders, and community inclusion are some of the approaches that connect beneficiaries with projects (Helfer 2006; Bassler et al. 2008; Arvelo 2012).

Various forms of development assistance in Bangladesh include those from international (foreign-aided projects), national (central government-development initiatives such as health, education and agriculture) and local levels (local government institutions at the village level). This chapter reveals how development assistance through projects with various goals relates the concept of BE to development participation and suggests the need for project management. As identified during fieldwork, having BE as a project component is essential for both GOs and NGOs to reach out to beneficiaries. Beneficiaries interact with organisations (GOs, NGOs) within project settings, and different phases of development projects lead to different types of beneficiary interactions. It is interesting to find out that communicating project benefits greatly impacts BE, which is critical to ensuring development participation. The following sections illustrate the findings in detail.

BE as a Project Component

As discussed in chapter two, BE occurs within government and NGO project settings. Projects are the main tools for GOs and NGOs to transfer policies on development participation into practises of engaging beneficiaries for many reasons. First, projects that include BE make it easier for GOs and NGOs to connect people to development interventions. For implementing agencies such as NGOs, having BE as a component in projects is critical to ensuring BE at different levels of the project management. Development assistance is provided to GOs and NGOs for projects and sector programs, although bilateral development partners also provide budgetary support to the government. Thus, engaging target groups in the process of implementing projects enables the organisations (mainly NGOs) to receive project funds. When projects are implemented, beneficiaries are selected as per project provisions, and BE strategies are outlined in the project goals and objectives, as identified in interviews with agriculture officials and NGOs who both connect to beneficiaries through projects. Once outlined in the project, it is easy to implement BE components. If BE is not included in the project document, it becomes difficult for NGOs to engage beneficiaries as it may contradict with the rules and procedures that they follow in carrying out development activities within the regulatory control of the government. NGOs operate within the legal framework of the government, and its various processes and steps of approval. Thus, having BE as a component in the project document makes it easier for NGOs to engage beneficiaries and ensure their participation around project activities.

In projects that are implemented by GOs, the responsibilities remain with these entities to ensure that beneficiaries are involved in development programs; for example, primary-education projects where the GOs have significant implementation responsibilities. The inclusion of beneficiaries is mentioned in the cooperation agreement, which is signed between the government department and schools under the project coverage. For projects that receive foreign funds, engagement directives already exist regarding the role of the government, beneficiaries, schools and the authorities, as revealed during an interview with an education officer. Apart from the usual roles and responsibilities of the DAE, engaging target-group beneficiaries – for example, farmers – takes place in a project setting. Discussions with research participants revealed that projects in this sector follow a group approach to BE, and groups comprise small and marginal farmers. Engaging beneficiaries occurs at different stages of project implementation such as crop production, disbursement of credit support, post-harvest management, marketing, value-chain creation and training.

Projects are critical for UPs to engage with beneficiaries as these local-government entities now have the expanded role of service delivery and inclusion of local people (see Fig. 2.4). An interview with a UP chairperson revealed that the project Local Government Support Programme Phase II is led by the government and the World Bank, where people's demands have been addressed through ward meetings. This project has components of ward meetings which, according to the UP chairperson, comprise the platform for people's participation in the local-development process. These provisions of ward meetings in the project document create the scope for BE within the project that UPs are implementing. Similarly, it is a requirement of the government's development planning and NGOs' own guidelines that projects lead to BE in the development field. As identified in the primary-data sources, both GOs and NGOs consider project components to be critical for BE and seem to be confident in engaging beneficiaries within the project setting. There is no contradiction between GO and NGO perceptions on this finding.

BE in practise depends on the type of project. While research participants claimed it is subject to project components, they did not confirm whether it has been included across all projects in the public sector, for example the electricity supply or other infrastructure projects. BE seems to be absent or limited in projects under the revenue budget,[20] as identified during the interviews. BE in the public sector is also subject to what budgetary option (revenue or development) is in place. It has been identified that beneficiaries are informed (rather than engaged at the outset) of these projects funded by the revenue budget only when they see the impact, either positive or negative. For example, people come to know about powerplants or other large projects when the media starts reporting on their negative or positive impacts. NGOs do not implement these projects. This may be a reason why BE is said to be an integral component of NGO projects, though BE within NGO project settings entails conditioning factors such as donor influence and the requirements of its funding. From this end, NGO projects appear to better integrate beneficiaries because funding falls under the development budget and donors prefer BE. These seem to be the key reasons associated with BE within the type and nature of projects in the NGO sector.

Compliance with Project Manuals and Templates

While it is revealed that project components enhance BE in development programs, it is important to note how far BE is subject to compliance with project templates and formats of reporting in the public sector, as mentioned by research participants. The development-project proforma (DPP) and technical assistance project proforma (TAPP) templates of the Planning Commission were examined to find out whether development projects in the public sector require BE. Examining the secondary sources revealed that the templates and formats used in the formality of project formulation and implementation are critical for incorporating provisions for engaging with beneficiaries in the first instance. Compliance with processes is an integral part of the project-management system (Too and Weaver 2014, 1389). Thus, compliance with BE provisions in project templates and formats naturally makes it easier to engage beneficiaries for their participation. A

[20] The revenue budget includes domestic receipts (e.g. tax, non-tax revenue), and the development budget is prepared for development activities inclusive of revenue surplus and private receipts (Banglapedia 2015).

desk review of secondary sources comprising project templates of GOs and NGOs, sample projects and project reports was conducted during the fieldwork to further investigate how BE is integrated into projects within GO–NGO project settings. The following sections highlight key findings from the secondary sources.

Requirements of project templates in the public sector

Development projects in investment or technical assistance categories need to align with the government's development policies, SDGs, individual ministry strategic plans and partner-countries' priorities (GOB 2016).[21] Following development planning and policies, technical-assistance projects in different ministries and service sectors formed the basis for BE, given the scope of project activities. It is evident that establishing the right content for project templates plays an important role in receiving approval for projects for implementation. The template provides broad categories of project costs for proposed consultancy services, human resources, seminars and training (GOB 2016, 15).

Beneficiary orientation of the DPP[22] is outlined in the project-description template, which includes a description of information regarding gender-segregated data, problems specific to women and the description of population coverage under the proposed project. The template also includes a description of project impacts on gender, women and children, disadvantaged groups of people and the community. The DPP Manual makes the project description inclusive of target beneficiaries, in that targets should be furnished in numbers and percentages to make the project consistent with its logical framework and sectoral priorities. Given the nature of projects, BE becomes part of reporting the project objectives, verifiable indicators and means of verification (GED 2014, Part A, 15). However, for the TAPP, project-description requirements, as mentioned in the circular, do not clarify the requirements of BE in the project template. It is difficult to understand from the template of the TAPP project-description requirements (Section 19) whether the expected outputs and outcomes imply a beneficiary orientation in terms of "trained manpower" (see GOB 2016, 93), although the project-implementation plan requires the description of issues relating to poverty, environment, climate change, women, children and gender.

[21] Section 6.1(a) of the Planning Division's Circular, issued on October 10, 2016.

[22] Development Project Proforma Manual, Part 2, Section 15, 15.6, and 24.

Requirements of project templates in the NGO sector

Examining the specific requirements of project templates for NGOs further expanded the findings identified from the primary-data sources. The NGOAB has a specific project template for NGOs that submit proposals for foreign funding called the FD-6 Template for Foreign Aided Projects. Paragraph 6(D) includes a table for displaying the main activities, allocation of funding against each activity and the number of target beneficiaries. The total number of beneficiaries is set against the total project funding, which is subject to the size and scope of the work of an NGO submitting a proposal for approval of funding (NGOAB n. d.).

The above findings from secondary data sources demonstrate that having beneficiaries integrated into the development activities occurs in the project design and components. The PKSF template clearly outlines the requirements for integrating communities and ensuring social inclusion in its project-appraisal policy: the Social Management Framework provides guidelines on community consultations with beneficiary groups, and project preparation guidelines include a section on target people or groups to describe how communities of the project area will be included (PKSF 2012a). Similarly, donors want a methodology for participant selection, which must be well defined with clarified criteria. An interview with an NGO official suggests that donors maintain the procedural aspects of aid management and the participatory approach to development while their programs are "only for those targeted."

These findings on compliance and fulfilling the requirements of templates reiterate that BE is not an "automatic" or "immediate" activity in development planning and projects, which is identified by Moser and Sollis (2006, 21) in their evaluation of community participation in a public-healthcare project in Ecuador. BE is a process within a government or NGO project setting with an objective of development participation. Thus, BE could be part of several important factors, including complying with project templates.

Project Interactions and Scope of BE

Given that both GOs and NGOs consider BE to be a component specific to the context of projects, it is also determined that interactions in project-management steps are critical for engaging beneficiaries. However, data in this connection also raised some key elements that research participants felt were equally important to finding the right context for BE. Engaging in a project responds to project-management cycles, organisational interaction and stakeholder coordination. Research participants mentioned that BE occurs mainly in the implementation phase. As shared by research participants, BE is subject to organisation–beneficiaries–project interrelationships in the total project-management cycle, which enables GOs and NGOs to engage with project beneficiaries. In addition, when it is a matter of project management, beneficiary context, project context, project type and liaising with local administration and UPs, everything needs to be considered for BE, as illustrated in the following sections.

Project context and priority

For the success of a project, the development context is significant. Each context varies and, even within a specific country, problem identification and project planning need to be taken into consideration (Ika and Donnelly 2017, 44). While engaging beneficiaries is integrated into project provisions, the specific context of development problems is identified, in line with development policies that intend to deliver services or benefits to communities. The development contexts differ in individual service sectors and are subject to the commitment and priorities of the higher authority, as noted by agriculture officials and a respondent from the DWA. While beneficiaries are expected to participate in all phases of a project,[23] it depends on the priority of projects, and as such the project that comes directly from the highest authority gets the highest priority, as mentioned by a research participant. For example, the agriculture sector has been receiving the highest level of political commitment that minimises the imposition of donor conditions. Agriculture projects receive priority from the highest authority of the government, which enables the inclusion of beneficiaries at all phases. Women's development and the inclusion of the women's workforce have been mainstreamed in Bangladesh; it seems that women's participation is integrated by default in the government or NGO development contexts. Thus, BE in the public sector responds to the priority of the project context that is beneficial for development participation.

The project context for NGOs falls within the scope of their work[24] and the priorities of the government or funding organisation, such as donors. NGOs study the policies of GOs and determine gaps between the policies and requirements of the Human Development Index (HDI) to develop them into funding opportunities, which leads to project planning and implementation;

[23] In a broad sense, it covers planning, implementation and evaluation.

[24] Clause 10 of the Foreign Donations (Voluntary Activities) Regulation Act 2016 describes several areas that NGOs work in Bangladesh.

they respond to donor expectations, depending on what funding agencies (either donors or GOs) are intending to provide for; and they try to relate the gaps to what funding is available, as revealed during an interview with an NGO official. GOs' development priority is beneficial for NGOs addressing social and human development, as is evident in interviews with NGO staff. Similar information was identified in FGDs with NGO respondents, which demonstrated that work with minority ethnic communities in the northern part of the country ultimately obtained government priority that made engaging the Dalit[25] community within an NGO project successful. The FGDs revealed that the project on this ethnic-minority group that works for social inclusion through the standardisation of living received attention, and the Dalit representation in the project event was instrumental to convincing the government to carry the project further. Therefore, it is not only the development planning and policies that can create the project context for BE; responding to priorities, addressing development gaps and conveying these to the government also create project components on BE in the development context of Bangladesh.

Project agreements and resources

GOs and NGOs have development agreements with donors or GOs and NGOs that outline activities and guidelines for participation that research participants consider important for BE in project settings. The agreements also form the basis for the human and financial resources required to deliver services to the target population and engage communities in development activities. Development activities intend to deliver services to the community, which requires both financial resources and human skills to manage and deliver them. Interviews with a project staff member and an NGO official revealed that funding guarantees staff to reach beneficiaries, and engagement starts when the project funds are received. Therefore, agreements and resources play an important role for GOs and NGOs engaging beneficiaries because they are important for GOs or NGOs to implementation projects.

[25] A low-caste, marginalised and deprived community working in dire conditions with the lowest labour costs. The literal meaning of Dalit is "deprived" (Banglapedia online).

Achievements and continuation

Beneficiaries can provide feedback on whether a problem has been resolved or services delivered within a project setting. This phase covers the evaluation part, in which beneficiaries are engaged to assess the progress and achievements of projects. This is related to the project lifecycle, which is critical for GOs and NGOs to either continue it or handover to communities. For NGOs, it also indicates transferring project achievements to GOs to continue or replicate in other development interventions. Fig. 3.1 illustrates the critical aspects of project interactions with beneficiaries that were inevitable in the process of engaging them.

Fig. 3.1 displays the relationship between organisations (i.e. GOs, NGOs or project-management units), contexts and beneficiaries to deliver projects to target populations. Organisations and beneficiaries carry the same importance in linking each of the project-management stages within and between organisations and the communities. According to Abraham (2014, 1), regardless of project type, a step in the project-management cycle "links with the proceedings and leads forward to the next one." The absence of any of these elements may weaken interactions between projects and beneficiaries, which was identified in research interviews (see Fig. 3.1). To discuss the management of project management, Too and Weaver (2013, 1384) provide a diagram to display elements of organisational governance, which includes addressing change, people in organisations, finances, future aspects and relations with stakeholders and communities, which are interrelated. According to the authors, none of these elements operate in isolation and any disconnect will impact other elements and the organisation. Similarly, BE is perceived by research participants as an interrelated aspect of project management, which does not automatically happen in GOs or NGOs. Thus, development participation is an outcome of all these interactions taking place for BE within project management.

Fig. 3.1. Interactions of organisations and beneficiaries in project management

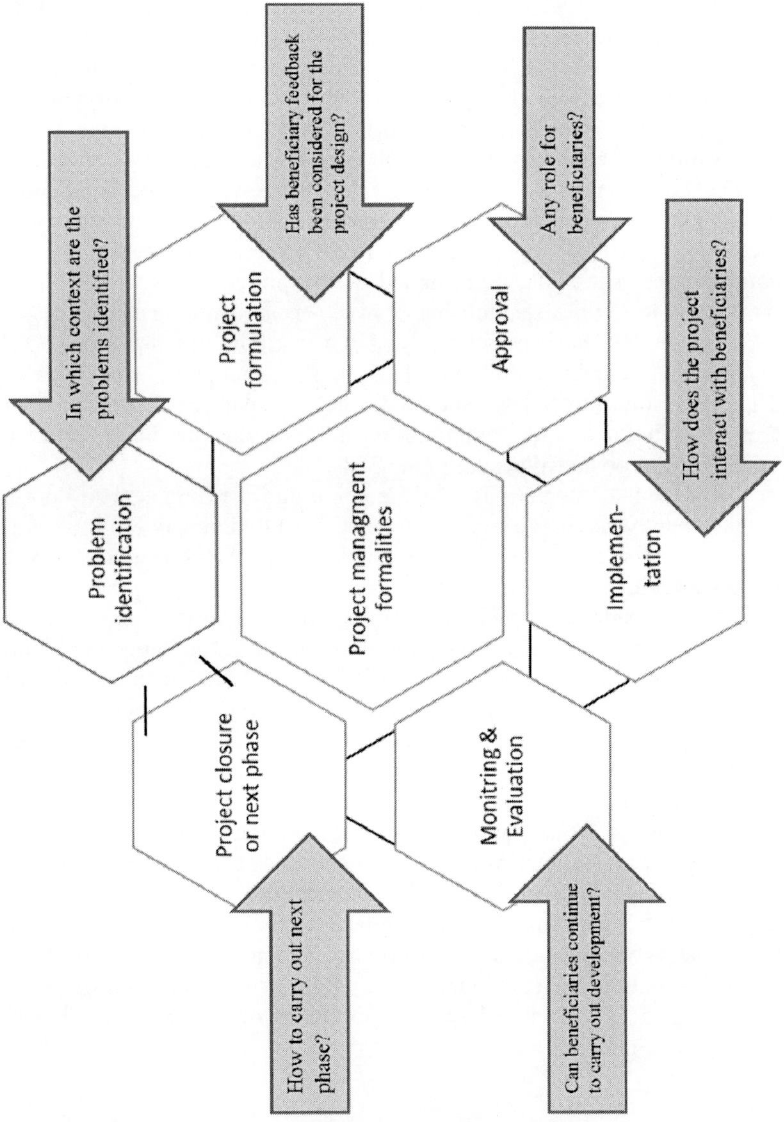

Source: Dutta (2021a), adapted from Abraham (2014, 1–3)

Beneficiary Interactions Within Project Management

Project–beneficiary interactions are seen as "tripartite interactions" between GOs, NGOs and beneficiaries. Different project-management and coordination committees have representation from GOs, including UPs, NGOs and project beneficiaries. These committees make up the platform through which communities get the opportunity to talk to representatives from GOs and NGOs about advantages, disadvantages, problems and their requirements. For example, the village-development committee in the UP is represented by local communities, in which direct interactions with project beneficiaries occur. The union-development coordination committee also holds monthly meetings, at which representatives from project beneficiaries or local communities participate as designed in the project work plan. The key purpose is to build a relationship between these committees representing GOs and/or NGOs, beneficiaries and the communities that leads to the management of projects from problem identification to evaluation (see Fig. 3.1). As organisations, GOs and NGOs need to manage relationships with their stakeholders and communities and not operate in isolation (as identified in Too and Weaver 2014, 1384).

Institutional interactions with communities are related to project management where BE initially occurs in consultation between project and community representatives, which enables the provision of feedback for implementation. These interaction strategies for engaging beneficiaries generate a "feedback system" to identify problems in the community that leads to "corrective actions" to resolving problems (Nakibinge et al. 2009, 192). Primary-data sources as identified in this study included different activities generating interactions between GOs, NGOs and beneficiaries at different stages of the project-management cycle (see Fig. 3.2). Beneficiaries are engaged in planning, implementation and evaluation phases through these several interactive activities undertaken by GOs or NGOs within the project settings. Thus, development participation occurs when GOs or NGOs engage beneficiaries through collecting data, conducting household surveys and identifying development problems at the planning stage. A large part of participation takes place during implementation when beneficiaries are engaged through training, income generation, consultation or service delivery. Beneficiary participation can be achieved during the evaluation phase when they have the opportunity to provide feedback on the development interventions.

Fig. 3.2. Interactive activities for BE in project management

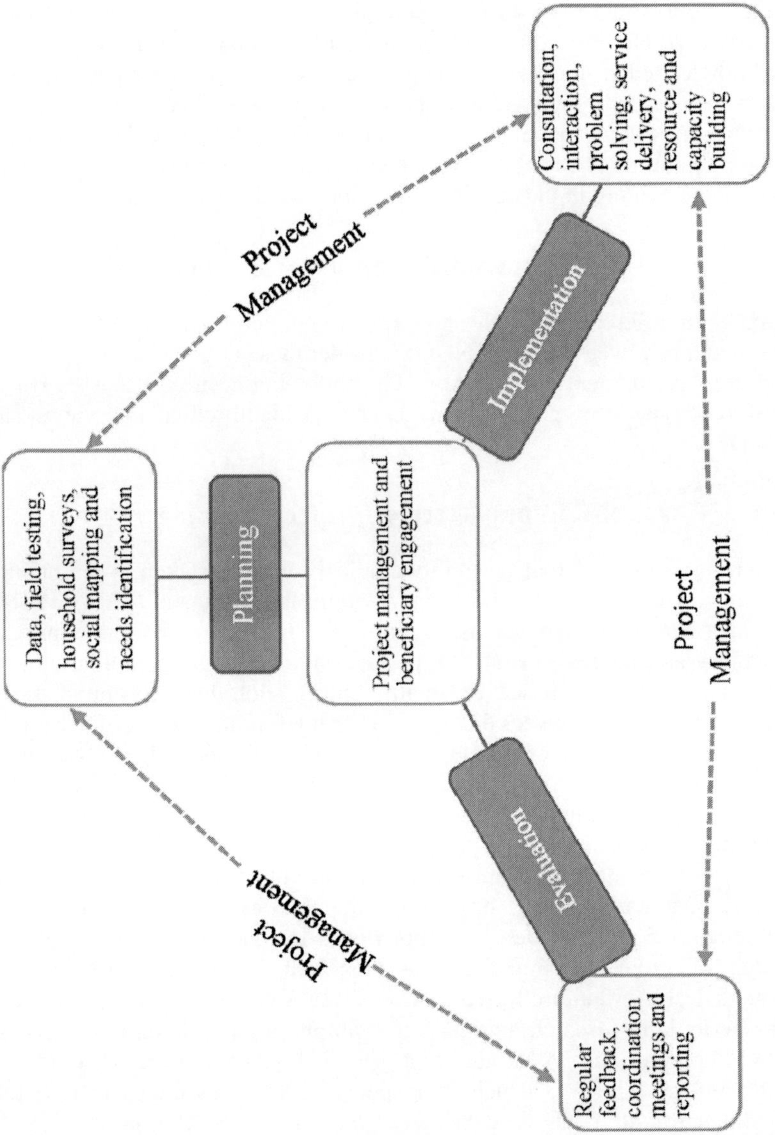

Source: Dutta (2021a)

Despite these project-management arrangements, there could be insufficient conditions to build relationships because each of these conditions cannot perform on its own without links to other conditioning factors (Turner 2004, 349). In addition, although engagement is desired and acknowledged in the development field to ensure people's participation, questions remain, such as "why, how, who and when" engagement occurs during project management (Moser and Sollis 2006, 19). The following findings outline BE in three basic steps of the project-management cycle, which are evident in the development context of Bangladesh.

Engaging from Planning to Evaluation

There are different approaches to BE within government and NGO-project contexts; however, GOs and NGOs consider these approaches as critical to ensure development participation. The following section discusses BE in different phases of project management as identified in interviews and FGDs.

BE in public-sector project planning

Interviews revealed that feasibility studies were undertaken in the public-sector investment and infrastructure projects. Abraham (2014, 13–14) defines feasibility studies as preliminary studies to determine project viability and address changes in project environments, including cultural and social changes based on quality information for decision making. However, the interviewees did not claim that BE is an element of feasibility studies for public sector development projects, such as bridge construction or capital projects. Since these kinds of projects were not included for research investigation, the discussion in this book does not focus on any feasibility studies. However, participants revealed that BE occurs in service-sector development programs, in which baseline studies, collecting field-level quantitative data on target populations and feedback from beneficiaries are considered as approaches for participation in the initial stage of project formulation. As identified by a DAE official, the Bangladesh Agriculture Research Council (BARC) organises field trials of the agriculture research outputs (for example, high yielding crops, seeds, etc.) with farmers. After the trials, BARC sends the feedback to the Agriculture Ministry, which is responsible for providing the research findings to the DAE to distribute them to farmers for production, if approved. Thus, development participation is expected while farmers are engaged in testing the new crop production. In addition, any large-scale agriculture production decided by the Ministry is subject to beneficiary concurrence, as the farmer's opinion is the basic requirement for continuing cultivation. In this sector, project planning is based on information that departmental officials obtain from farmers – an approach that ensures their participation.

However, this strategy is not applied in the same way across other service sectors, in which public-sector officials may not need to talk directly to beneficiaries to identify their needs. In such cases, the national database on field research created by health professionals and researchers is a strategy for BE in health-project planning. For example, the statistics on child mortality or the maternal mortality rate should lead to projects on child nutrition or safe motherhood, which is reflected in the national database available from the Department of Health. Here, data are mainly quantitative and scientific. However, an interview with the UH&FPO in this sector raised the question of how far BE is integrated across development programs in this service sector that allows beneficiary participation. There is bureaucracy in program design and planning, and engaging field-level staff is not adequate. The interviewee felt that there is always a professional gap between field-level officers and the officials at the central level, and information from field-level officials may not always be considered for the development agenda at the national level.

NGO sector project planning and BE

Project planning appears to be different in the NGO sector, in which the identification of needs, social mapping and household surveys are mandatory tools for engaging with beneficiaries during the planning stage. In addition, visits to project areas and face-to-face interactions with beneficiaries enable social mapping to identify development issues and assess project needs based on information directly obtained from beneficiaries. Interviews with NGO fieldworkers identified that they visit individual households on a regular basis and talk to people who are not existing beneficiaries. This interaction helps them identify new beneficiary needs that can generate new project plans in specific geographical locations. This process of engaging beneficiaries appears to be the same across NGOs working in different areas and implementing different development programs. For example, an interview with an NGO fieldworker in the northern part of Bangladesh revealed similar findings. For that NGO, the engagement process starts with a social-wellbeing mapping analysis before the formulation of a project and identification of the beneficiaries. NGOs also conduct a baseline survey to engage beneficiaries. Social mapping identifies the resources available in a specific area and how to link resources identified in social mapping with the government's development programs. This NGO approach to BE is based on assessing needs and beneficiary identification for a certain project. For NGOs, it does not matter what type of project they undertake because BE is a mandatory component.

Project planning is followed by project formulation and the approval process, in which professional expertise regarding project design is more important than BE, which was identified in the primary and secondary data sources. GOs and NGOs engage stakeholders in project design. In the public sector, concerned ministries or departments formulate projects in consultation with think tanks, NGOs and a cross section of professional groups. NGO project design follows the same way of engaging stakeholders and includes GOs, which was evident in several interviews. In both cases, if the project receives foreign funding, donors are involved in the design phase, for example through consultations with GOs, verifying NGO interactions with beneficiaries (see Fig. 2.4) and establishing development agreements or contracts. Different agencies in the public sector remain responsible for approval of the project size in terms of total project cost. NGO projects that receive foreign funding require NGOAB approval. If NGOs receive local funding, projects are approved by the Department of Social Services. Aligning with requirements is critical for receiving funding and commencing BE, along with other project components.

BE in the project implementation phase

BE must be a project component, and that engagement is largely undertaken during the implementation phase of project management, as discussed earlier in this chapter. This is because implementation is the stage during which most project activities take place (Abraham 2014, 3), and for this reason, project implementation is the critical phase for engaging beneficiaries. The implementation stage includes beneficiaries in project activities through gaining access to services, obtaining skills and knowledge on income-generation activities, or being empowered to raise their voices for a common social need, such as the development of marginalised groups of people. The following sections discuss a broad range of strategies to engage beneficiaries during the project-implementation phase.

Service delivery and BE

Respondents from different government departments at the central and field levels described the delivery of services under development projects as a way to engage citizens who are the main users of public services, for example, health, education, agriculture, livestock and local development. Note that not all service provisions are outlined in projects alone; these are public services that citizens receive as right holders. Some of the public-sector development programs like agriculture, health or education include the provision of services within projects that requires engaging beneficiaries for their participation. Interviewees from NGOs perceived BE to be the key element to ensure access to services. During project implementation, individual departments remain responsible for informing target beneficiaries of the intended benefits of services. Therefore, BE during the implementation of projects implies conveying development information to people or target groups and delivering services. To some extent, this is beyond the traditional methods of delivering services, which was observed by the UH&FPO. To him, doctors are there for more than providing treatment alone; they need to have skills to reach people and inform them about developments in the health sector, which needs door-to-door visits to engage beneficiaries. For example, there may be problems prevailing in the community that health services need to address and raise awareness to prevent. An informal discussion with a doctor working at an Upazila revealed that the number of female patients (in rural areas) attempting suicide is one of the main reasons for hospitalisation. Here BE is required for prevention rather than the usual treatment. It does not happen outside the scope of the project: service delivery is what the treatment can provide.

BE in development programs requires multiple strategies and options to deliver services to communities, especially in the health sector. There needs to be synchronised engagement activities that are related to the purpose of development programs, as identified in the interview with the UH&FPO. Nakibinge et al. (2009, 192–3) identified how a comprehensive set of multiple-engagement activities comprising clinical care, healthcare promotion, sports and commemoration of national days to "improve the social interaction and cohesion" in the community led to its engagement in the context of a health-research project in Uganda. However, whether the health sector in Bangladesh addresses these broad spectrums of development to engage beneficiaries cannot be discerned from interviews, though communicating health concerns and project benefits remains in practice in this context. An interview with a UP chairperson revealed that engagement comprises the provision of multiple services beyond the traditional function of participating in elections every five years. It is the provision of services that encourages communities to remain in touch with the UP and access the required services. In recent times, UPs are expected to deliver services such as birth registration, citizenship certificate and verification to combat terrorist activities, for which people need to come to the UP. The ICT program is a new area of work in UPs where rural people come for training in computer skills in email, downloading and filling out passport forms, getting exam results and information regarding land records that people need. These service provisions create opportunities for rural people to be more engaged in development programs at the union level.

Service delivery for engaging beneficiaries requires strategies to ensure people's access to services, and the creation of provisions in the UP brings communities closer to development initiatives. In addition, when the government undertakes initiatives for infrastructure development for service delivery, such as community-health services or education institutions for rural communities, engagement begins with wealthy people who may not reside in those areas but have connections through businesses, properties or kinship. The UP chairperson revealed that engaging in the establishment of a primary school in his constituency had multiple requirements: engaging a rich family for land, infrastructure establishment, the payment of salaries for a designated teacher and learning materials for children, and engaging parents to send their children to the school. Engagement is here subject to the personal connections of the UP chairperson, their accessibility to the community and the willingness of parents to send their children to that school, which are considered as comprising the participation of rural communities in this development intervention.

For NGOs, this is mainly covered by advocacy and campaigns that mobilise target beneficiaries for common understanding, which commence during project launch and continue until completion. NGOs do not have the authority to directly deliver services to people unless it is specifically mentioned in their project-implementation guidelines. However, they establish links between target beneficiaries and service providers in project areas. NGO fieldworkers believe that to gain access to services, beneficiaries need to be linked with government departments such as the Social Services Directorate and Directorate of Youth Development or land office. Following social mapping, NGO staff realise which institutions the beneficiaries need to be linked with. NGO fieldworkers visit target beneficiaries, listen to their requirements and assist them in contacting different institutions, such as the land office, livestock office or institutions that provide legal services. NGO fieldworkers also coordinate with various departments to obtain required information for beneficiaries, which was identified in several interviews.

Capacity development and BE

Capacity development is one of the major strategies through which GOs and NGOs engage beneficiaries during the project-implementation phase. It contributes to the development of beneficiary skills, which leads to their income generation, financial stability and social enhancement in rural areas (Lusthaus, Adrien and Perstinger 1999; Merino and Carmenado 2012). In the views of research participants, training is an important project activity to engage beneficiaries. Primary-data sources revealed that GOs and NGOs engage project beneficiaries through training and skills-development activities. This is specialised skills-based training, such as promoting health workers for community clinics, computing, demonstrations of new technologies for cultivation and other livelihood activities, including raising poultry and livestock for income generation, as revealed during interviews and the FGD with beneficiaries.

According to research participants, capacity development appears to be the basis for BE because this leads to income-generation activities for poverty reduction, which is the prime focus of development policies. Engagement is critical because mobilising beneficiaries for training and demonstrations is subject to convincing them. It was identified during interviews and FGDs that GOs and NGOs need to demonstrate how projects or training opportunities benefit people in terms of providing the skills required for income generation or improvements in their social and economic conditions. Interviews and FGDs with NGOs also revealed that beneficiaries do not always voluntarily join capacity-development activities, in which case NGO fieldworkers need to identify the right tool for BE. The critical aspect is to bring them in and get them involved in project activities, which requires engagement and conveying the appropriate messages of the project benefits to communities. Findings from interviews revealed that it is important to make beneficiaries understand the benefits and positive sides of the project. For example, farmers will not accept the new crop or technology unless they see the benefits of these interventions. Box 2 (based on the FGD with NGOs) reveals the practical experiences of NGO fieldworkers who tried to mobilise young people for capacity-development training in the project area.

Box 2. Talking face-to-face to engage beneficiaries

This practical experience is related to the formal publicity of a project on training, skill development and income generation in a district in the northern part of Bangladesh. The NGO distributed project leaflets on training programs among people in the project area. However, the responses from people on participating in the training programs did not meet the expectation and target of the program, so NGO staff decided to talk to people. They were divided into groups and sat in local tea stalls, community gathering places and hat-bazars (rural open marketplaces) to talk to elderly people and discuss the benefits (generation of employment, better income because of technical and ICT skills, etc.) of the training programs. Following this initiative, responses to the project participation were higher. People gained the confidence to send their young family members to the training, and the problem of non-participation was minimised.

Respondents from GOs and NGOs said that they sometime experience difficulties in engaging women beneficiaries, for which identifying the appropriate approach to reaching out is essential. Although advocacy of NGOs helped to raise awareness of women's participation in capacity building and other development activities, as recognised in interviews with participants from the DWA, social barriers still make it difficult to ensure that women are involved in non-traditional work. For example, there are challenges to engaging women in farming activities due to the social and cultural contexts of rural areas, which are mostly conservative. It is important to note that rural people, including women in Bangladesh, are familiar with agriculture and farming; however, involving them in any specific government or NGO project on agriculture requires extra effort. In such cases, engaging beneficiaries begins with the male members of the family, who are not project beneficiaries directly. An informal discussion with an NGO executive revealed that the organisation once arranged field visits for male members of families to see the project outcome in other areas. This approach helped to enhance their confidence and ensure the female members participated in the project activities specifically designed for women's capacity development. Although capacity-development activities cover the major strategies of beneficiary engagement, individual contexts and circumstances lead GOs and NGOs to determine engagement strategies. However, they mainly provide training, which was evident in the public sector, and NGO staff identified various other methods to mobilise beneficiaries for capacity-development programs.

Financial resources and BE

One of the major purposes of engaging beneficiaries is building individual capacity (discussed above) so they can participate in development activities, contribute to local-development programs, integrate marginalised communities with mainstream development programs and undertake income-generation activities. Interviews with GOs and NGOs revealed that individual beneficiary capacity is enhanced through transferring skills such as training and providing financial resources (microcredit or small loans) to beneficiaries. Microcredit interventions in the lives of the rural poor in Bangladesh are said to be instrumental in creating the gradual enhancement of "peace through economic inclusion," rather than any radical movement for social change (Cons and Paprocki 2010, 640). The provision of microcredits or small loans, as mentioned by research participants, enables beneficiaries, especially women, to improve their economic and social conditions, and ensure their participation in the development activities. Microcredit or small-loan provisions are now a reality in the rural people's capacity development in Bangladesh. NGO officials claimed that beneficiaries get access to money through microfinance, and poor people do so without mortgages,[26] which they think is a big achievement of NGOs. At the same time, money flow is important as people need capital for alternative income-generation activities. "Without microcredit, where would people get the capital from?" - the research participant asked.

While advocacy, campaigns and training develop knowledge and access to information, financial resources help project beneficiaries transform skills into income-generating activities and improve their social and economic conditions. It was evident from conversations with GOs, NGOs and beneficiaries that microcredit programs lead to BE in project management. Findings from interviews with NGOs demonstrated that having access to financial resources is critical for beneficiaries and has been recognised as a method of BE, in which the contribution of NGOs is significant. It is important to note that all beneficiaries interviewed or who attended the FGD had received small loans or microcredit from either NGO or government projects. NGOs provide microcredit for livelihood and income-generating activities, as do government-service-sector projects, such as agriculture projects. For example, three male farmers who were the direct project beneficiaries of an agriculture project and received loans for cultivation were interviewed. In addition, beneficiaries receive repeated loans or microcredit, depending on the expansion of their livelihood activities.

[26] Though the interest rate is higher than that for bank loans.

Fig. 3.3 illustrates how beneficiaries are engaged through repeated microcredit provisions. FGDs with beneficiaries revealed that financial resources were important for them to generate income to ensure family wellbeing. Women beneficiaries participate in development programs, such as small entrepreneurship. They have small-scale businesses, including handmade shopping bags, tailoring, poultry, livestock and homemade dairy products, for which they receive NGO training. The capacity development and wellbeing of beneficiaries are closely linked in implementing the microcredit component of projects and funding beneficiaries in the family and community. The marginalised groups, for example the Dalit community, also receive small loans and income generation from poultry or livestock, which helps them to send their kids to schools, which was not previously possible. For beneficiaries, it is important to have capital to continue their entrepreneurship and income-generation activities while they receive the required skills during project implementation. BE through projects ensures their participation in these development activities. An NGO executive claimed during an interview that NGOs succeed in ensuring participation as BE is integral to microcredit provisions. This is difficult for public-sector banks as they cannot maintain regular interaction with beneficiaries and monitoring the progress daily after disbursing loans, which NGOs do within project areas.

Fig. 3.3. Relationship between microcredit and BE

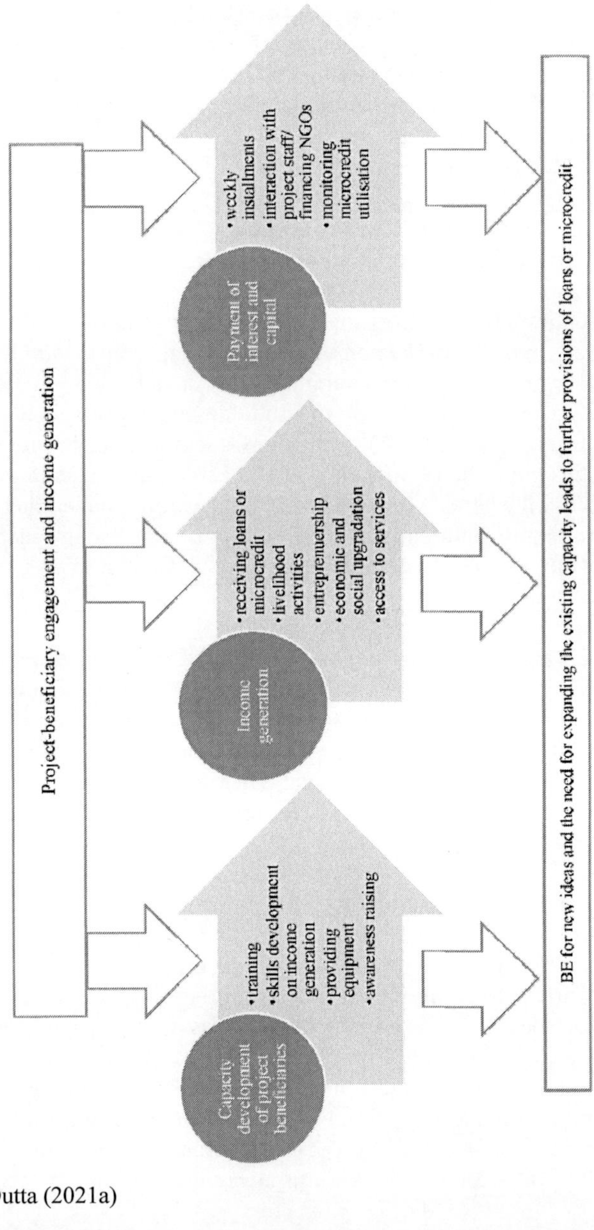

Source: Dutta (2021a)

Awareness raising and BE

Apart from financial resources, project beneficiaries are also engaged through awareness raising, which is integrated into community-empowerment programs during the implementation of projects. This is evident in the development of the Dalit community, as revealed during a FGD with project beneficiaries, including Dalit representatives from the northern part of Bangladesh (see Box 3).

Box 3. BE and community harmony

Women from the Dalit community were engaged in capacity development under an NGO-implemented project. Additionally, the broader community comprising people from Hindu and Muslim communities and a cross section of others was engaged to build positive attitudes towards the Dalit community. Previously, people from this community were not able to talk to Hindu or Muslim people because of their identity and caste. Now this division is less visible; people from all communities go to their houses and attend ceremonies, and Dalit people can also go anywhere. According to a Dalit woman beneficiary, when they learn skills and earn a livelihood through income-generating activities, they can get married and have equal rights and a voice in the family and community.

However, the FGD with NGO staff revealed that raising awareness in human rights-based projects like the one for the Dalit community was not enough for BE; it also requires establishing the connection between grassroots-level community-development activities with policymakers to demonstrate the need for development. Therefore, it is engaging with not only project beneficiaries but also government departments in Bangladesh to support policy interventions for the development of ethnic-minority communities. Additionally, the media is an important stakeholder in spreading the achievements of development activities, as discussed during the FGD.

Engaging beneficiaries through the provision of microcredit by NGOs includes awareness raising on various social, health and education issues. At the grassroots level, NGO officials discuss various awareness issues written in the credit-interest register while collecting weekly interest repayments in a specific project area. NGO staff discuss many issues that are relevant to their everyday life, for example campaigning for health and hygiene, immunisation or anti-dowry issues. Since the concerned NGOs do not conduct further research on how this awareness raising impacts the lives of beneficiaries, it is difficult to say whether it is enabling beneficiaries to participate in broader development issues, for example maintaining health and hygiene, resisting child marriage, or eliminating dowry provisions causing domestic violence. However, it also cannot be claimed that BE through awareness raising does not have any impact on development participation, as the Dalit example (see Box 3) reveals that communities from different religious and caste groups do not hesitate to interact with them.

Awareness raising is critical in public-sector development programs, such as health programs that target poor and vulnerable groups. Staff shortages in field-level health offices are evident, whereas engaging beneficiaries needs regular interactions. BE is the key focus of the government in the implementation of primary-education projects in Bangladesh, including schools, students and parents. However, the education sector is divided into various streams. BE needs to focus on beneficiary needs. When the approach is too diverse, it gives rise to various requirements of beneficiaries, and, given their diverse needs and background, this makes their synchronised engagement difficult, as mentioned in an interview with a development partner. One of the participants mentioned in a seminar that if the development interventions are too diverse, they result in less engaged beneficiaries and therefore inadequate participation.

BE in monitoring and evaluation (M&E)

Project monitoring is an ongoing activity throughout the project lifecycle, which occurs monthly, quarterly and annually. Project-implementation agencies such as GOs, including UPs and NGOs, donors (if foreign-funded) and relevant institutions from service sectors, participate in the M&E of projects. GOs and NGOs attempt to ensure the participation of stakeholders in the M&E phase. In this phase of project management, BE is guided by M&E formats of the GOs and NGOs and the reporting templates that donors have. GOs and NGOs need to comply with M&E requirements and templates as an integral part of the project-management cycle. For example, an NGO that receives grants from PKSF is guided by its M&E tools, and PKSF monitors project implementation. Government monitoring also occurs when NGOs receive funding directly from the government and implement projects. Engaging project beneficiaries is stated in the M&E guidelines of the PKSF, according to which the responsible staff need to ensure that a cross section of communities, including teachers, elected representatives and social elites, participate in the process to provide feedback on development activities. Information obtained from their participation provides input for the reporting that the PKSF and partner NGO require (see PKSF 2012b).

M&E is integrated into projects undertaken by GOs and NGOs and is required for BE. For example, project management in the public sector adopts M&E tools and techniques of project monitoring and develops M&E templates for use in project management, such as the Logical Framework Matrix (LFM), a reporting tool which is outlined in the DPP Manual. Engagement is implied by "network reports," although it is not spelled out in these monitoring tools (see GED 2014, 22–5). More clarifications on how beneficiaries are involved in M&E may be required in the Technical Assistance[27] (TA) project-implementation processes. BE for participation of the community in M&E occurs during field-level implementation in certain public-sector development projects. It appears that the local-government development programs integrate communities in monitoring-development programs. Box 4 demonstrates how communities are engaged in M&E, as identified by NGO participants during the FGD.

Box 4. Engaging communities in public-sector procurement

The infrastructure work is done by the LGED[28] at the UPZ level. There are development works undertaken by government departments like the Upazila Health Complex or Education Department. The community needs to be aware of development projects that various departments of the government implement at the field level and participate in identifying merits of public works. Here NGOs link communities with the LGED. The community monitors whether the construction work is in line with the plan. The LGED cannot change the design of the infrastructure of the original plan because it needs to show the design to the people, who in turn need to agree to it. The LGED also needs to declare the award of the contract, as per the citizens' charter of the department. This is how the community is participating while having this monitoring role.

Based on the above case, it is difficult to claim that beneficiaries are engaged in project M&E across the public sector, because BE is subject to project type and component. How far rural communities are aware of the construction design and plan is a question of whether NGOs with specialised knowledge are assisting the community in monitoring these projects. It is

[27] Defined in Appendix A

[28] The Local Government Engineering Division, responsible for expediting the rural economy through transportation and market development. See www.lged.gov.bd.

not only about engaging beneficiaries in M&E but also about the need to ensure the credibility of implementation agencies in reaching out to the communities.

It is important for donors to monitor whether the right section of the population is targeted for development initiatives, whether templates for beneficiary participation are followed, and whether cooperation agreements made with the government or contracts with NGOs reflect deliverables for beneficiaries. Donors are required to ensure their own M&E or quality assurance. When NGOs provide the addresses of target beneficiaries, apps (for example Google Maps) facilitate the donor-monitoring process because individual donors will go directly to beneficiaries to determine the authenticity of the beneficiary inclusion (see Fig. 2.3). When NGOs are the implementing partners for donors taking project benefits to the beneficiaries, it is equally important that donors have monitoring mechanisms in place to ensure that partnerships exist between donors and NGOs, and between NGOs and beneficiaries.

Development Communication for BE

The driving force of development communication (DevCom) theories is focused on people, their social, behavioural and cultural contexts, and communication efforts to bring about social changes in which people are the main actors. The theory of Development Support Communication (DSC) advocates that development interventions should bridge project implementation and the responses of beneficiaries to make communication supportive of development (McAnany 2012). This provides beneficiaries a platform to receive and respond to development communication and participate in development activities. Failure to inform beneficiaries about development goals reduces their participation, and thus DSC is a way of promoting participation within institutional development planning (McAnany 2012). Communication and interaction are important tools for engaging beneficiaries within GO–NGO project settings. Multiple factors facilitate BE, such as development projects in the service sectors, human resources, financial resources and donor conditions. To this, development communication is critical in bringing beneficiaries on board, for which communicating development benefits is instrumental in ensuring beneficiary participation in development interventions.

DevCom and beneficiary responses within projects

Given that both GOs and NGOs consider BE for development participation specific to project contexts, interactions in project settings are critical for materialising this approach. Engaging beneficiaries in a project involves campaign, dialogue, awareness-raising activities, demonstrations, workshops and, most importantly, individual interactions. Both GOs and NGOs consider that interacting and communicating the project benefits are critical for engagement. DevCom approaches to BE encompass outreach to and interactions with beneficiaries.[29] Development participation is ensured through communicating development information to beneficiaries.

However, apart from reaching out and interactions within project settings, BE is also subject to how beneficiaries respond to information they receive through development communication. The FGD and interviews with beneficiaries revealed that the accessibility of information from field offices and NGOs, including their ability to communicate with staff and obtain services, creates an opportunity for them to be involved in project activities or GO–NGO programs (as discussed in chapter two). Access to mobile-phone networks significantly contributes to their access to information and services; for example, marketing the products they produce through small entrepreneurship has become easier due to the mobile network. Beneficiaries consider that receiving information directly from GOs or NGOs enables them to participate in project activities. Without the required information, beneficiaries find it difficult to connect with development interventions. Different approaches to communication occur at different phases of the project-management cycle and vary between projects and communities. The way that BE, through DevCom, is embedded in different phases of project management to ensure development participation is explained in Table 3.1. Beneficiary responses to DevCom are categorised according to the requirements of the different phases of project management.

[29] Appendix B details how beneficiary outreach and interactions are perceived as approaches to BE required for development participation.

Table 3.1. Beneficiary responses to DevCom within project settings

Project phases	BE practises	Beneficiary responses to participate
Planning	Need assessments, social mapping on beneficiary resources, data on education, and health	Conveying needs and providing information (e.g. health conditions) that lead to project formulation
Formulation	Formalities of project approval	–
Initiation	Project launch events	Beneficiaries are mobilised, attend events, and are informed of projects, impacts on lives and livelihoods
Implementation	Demonstration of project benefits (communication materials such as posters, flyers, arranging group discussions, and workshops), providing microcredits, training on income-generation activities, among others	Relates to their livelihoods – obtaining tangible outputs, generating income, and repaying interest, becoming group members, practicing social norms, maintaining health and hygiene, and having skills development
Monitoring and Evaluation	Obtaining feedback from beneficiaries, conducting surveys	Beneficiaries are expected to provide feedback

Source: Dutta (2021b)

It is important to note that these practises to a large extent differ between GO and NGO projects. For example, the agriculture sector has its staff at the field level that enables BE; however, shortages of doctors at the field level make it difficult to convey public-health information to beneficiaries, as identified by research participants. Despite different project settings or contextual differences, DevCom that addresses beneficiary contexts, beneficiary understanding and requirements are critical for engaging them for their participation in a local context.

Communicating development benefits

Interviews with government officials, NGO executives, fieldworkers and project-management staff revealed that they need to highlight project deliverables that relate to the socio-economic conditions of beneficiaries. The outcome of this approach largely depends on how beneficiaries perceive the benefits of development interventions, which vary in different development contexts, among men and women beneficiaries, and different socio-economic contexts. A couple of cases identified during FGDs with NGO participants and beneficiaries reflect different contexts of communicating development benefits for BE within a project context. Box 2 presents how talking face-to-face and convincing elderly family members resulted in beneficiary participation in the skill-development program. Interactions with beneficiaries must also demonstrate the benefits of a project to engage beneficiaries. To engage farmers in cultivating new crops or vegetables, the DAE officials had to demonstrate the yield. For example, a DAE demonstration in growing gourds convinced many farmers to participate in the project, which resulted in greatly improved production. An interview with a farmer, a member of the small farmers group under an agriculture project, revealed that he was not initially confident about the DAE, and doubted whether it would yield improved production or profit. However, he agreed to cultivate the vegetable after seeing the high-quality output, which was certainly profitable.

These two cases demonstrate that communicating development benefits as an approach to BE contributes to development participation if they are perceived as relevant by the beneficiaries. Simple communication materials like flyers or adopting farming equipment did not work for these two diverse groups of beneficiaries in either the GO or NGO project contexts. On the one hand, it required talking to individual beneficiaries to explain the benefits of training, while on the other the farmer continues vegetable production when they experience the tangible benefits of cultivation. In most cases, the development benefits are directly linked to livelihood, as is evident in microcredit programs (see Fig. 3.3).

Communication within communities

Communication is not limited to GOs, NGOs or project settings as the message spreading through the community can also convince people to participate in the project. Usually, small-scale loans or grants provided under certain social-development projects, such as income-generation projects or community-development projects, successfully engage beneficiaries through existing beneficiaries or the community in a local area. In such cases, information obtained from the next-door neighbour adds value. When asked how beneficiaries knew about the project that provides small-scale loans, one of the female beneficiaries, who had been living in dire poverty, said that obtaining information from neighbours on loans convinced her to contact NGO staff and start a small business, becoming involved in the project activities. Thus, for beneficiaries, it is critical to receive development information, and they respond when it relates to their socio-economic improvement.

The discussion in this chapter distinguishes between the strategies of GOs and NGOs in engaging project beneficiaries, and demonstrates how research participants perceived BE to be a deeply rooted element in development-project management associated with various conditioning factors. This chapter has revealed relevant critical issues in project management that GOs and NGOs consider essential to ensuring BE in the development process. The data also reveal how multiple factors exist in addressing BE, ranging from GO, NGO and donor policies to project-implementation practises and communicating development benefits. GOs and NGOs need to address these conditioning factors to ensure participation of beneficiaries in development projects. The discussion in this chapter creates the scope for investigating organisational strengths in engaging beneficiaries as GOs and NGOs engage beneficiaries in project-management settings. Thus, identifying the comparative advantages and limitations of GOs and NGOs fulfils this requirement, as presented in the next chapter.

CHAPTER FOUR

ADVANTAGES AND LIMITATIONS IN ENGAGING BENEFICIARIES

When BE is considered as a component of development projects and subject to interaction and communication with beneficiaries, GOs and NGOs experience advantages and limitations. There is no absolute advantage for any of these organisations; rather, one organisation considers the advantages of the other as opportunities for BE. However, NGOs seem to have more advantages than GOs, given their skills, expertise and beneficiary outreach in remote areas. GOs can equally attain these advantages if they have capacity at the field level. Sometimes, it is more the beneficiary's confidence in GOs than NGOs that puts GOs in a more advantageous position for engaging beneficiaries, though it is perceived that NGOs experience less limitations in comparison to GOs in reaching out to beneficiaries. Given the advantages and limitations, beneficiary choices matter for their participation in the development process that both GOs and NGOs need to address in engaging them.

Advantages of GOs and NGOs in BE

Research participants categorised advantages and limitations for GOs and NGOs into a few core themes, which enable or affect the GO–NGO scope of BE in the development process. As shown in Table 4.1, each of these core themes is based on several parameters on which the advantages of GOs and NGOs are determined. The data descriptions against each of the core themes were mentioned by research participants during interviews. These data also demonstrate the elements of advantages that are applicable to GOs and NGOs in the development field.

Table 4.1. Factors related to GO–NGO advantages for BE

Core themes of advantages	Data descriptions in brief	Advantages for GOs	Advantages for NGOs
Skills and expertise to engage	Training and skills specific to beneficiary engagement		√
	Specialised knowledge and skills like health professionals or agriculturists	√	
	Skills on beneficiary assessment, social mapping, communication/interaction		√
	Monitoring and evaluation skills		√
	Microcredit management skills		√
Job requirements	Skill-based recruitment		√
	Beneficiary engagement affecting jobs		√
	Recognition for beneficiary engagement		√
Outreach to beneficiaries	Door-to-door visits to beneficiaries		√
	Engaging women beneficiaries		√
	Engagement through nationwide LGIs	√	
	Project implementation staff in remote or difficult-to-reach areas		√
	Wider inclusion in service-sector development	√	
	Communicating project benefits		√
Authority	Approval of funding and projects	√	
	Enforceability (issuance of letters/memos)	√	
	Leading management and coordination committees	√	
	Representation in the committees	√	√

Beneficiary confidence	Meant to be accountable to people	√	
	Main stakeholder for development	√	
Advocacy	Project launch and information	√	√
	Interaction with beneficiaries	√	√
	Mobilising beneficiary participation		√

There are some areas identified for GOs and NGOs which suggest that one of these organisations is comparatively more advantageous than the other in engaging project beneficiaries. The following section elaborates these core themes of GO–NGO advantages that are critical for engaging beneficiaries.

Skills and Expertise for Engaging Project Beneficiaries

Skills and expertise for engaging beneficiaries are closely linked with capacity at the individual level obtained through training and learning opportunities within organisations. Training and capacity-development opportunities for staff in organisations influence the mobilising of project beneficiaries more than the individual capacity of beneficiaries to participate in project activities. The skills and expertise of GO and NGO staff are essential for building the capacity of beneficiaries and ensuring their participation in the project management. Therefore, the primary requirement of BE is to have staff capacity within organisations to engage, followed by the individual capacity of beneficiaries to participate. Because of the nature of the work, the staff capacity for engaging beneficiaries is more evident in NGOs than in GOs.

In an analysis of a Bangladeshi NGO's role in involving beneficiaries for participation, Harland (1991) claims that the staff responsible for engagement are the change agents who initiate participatory processes, which include dialogue, training and education for individuals and both small and large groups. The question is whether GOs in the development context of Bangladesh hold the skills and ability to engage beneficiaries, or if these are attributed only to NGOs. In relation to skills and the ability to engage, research participants considered the purpose of training for GOs and NGOs, expertise in M&E, expertise in microcredit management and access to financial resources to be the key factors that enable GOs or NGOs to engage project beneficiaries.

Staff skills specific to BE

NGO officials are comparatively skilled in engaging project beneficiaries because they are exposed to relevant training. NGO staff and fieldworkers receive hands-on training at the local level on different aspects of participatory methods, which enables them to engage beneficiaries through interactions. In describing the success of NGOs, Sarker (2005, 260) argues that one of the strategies is investment in human-resource development and recognising the significance of investment in staff expertise and systems required to "support field activities." NGO fieldworkers in Bangladesh also receive hands-on training relevant to engaging beneficiaries at the field level. Interviews with two female NGO fieldworkers in a northern district in Bangladesh revealed that they receive training on: women's empowerment, early childhood care development, advocacy, how to engage the private sector, disaster management, the project-implementation plan, the human rights-based approach (that prohibits and eliminates any form of discrimination), project management and sustainable development, participatory reflection and action,[30] the social mapping of beneficiary resources, wellbeing analysis and the community-action plan, which are directly related to BE.

Officials from government departments agreed that NGOs' capacity development is different from that of public-sector training, and that NGOs are in an advantageous position due to their staff capacity and skills in BE. They consider that NGO training is beneficiary oriented and, in contrast, public-sector training is resourceful. There are more training opportunities for GOs than NGOs because government officials can access foreign training. This implies that public-sector officials have greater scope to access training, although it may not be specific to BE or project issues. It is important to note that no research has been done to investigate how public-sector training is applicable in the development field, and whether it addresses the local context to integrate people into development. Despite not having significant foreign exposure, training for NGO staff members is largely local and based on local needs, which is an essential factor for development participation.

Specialised expertise to engage beneficiaries

Although the skills of BE are mainly attributed to NGOs, GOs have more advantages than NGOs in engaging those who require technical

[30] Working with communities (poor and marginalised) and enabling communities to analyse their own problems.

specialisationsfor example agriculturists for agriculture projects or medical professionals for health projects. In the agriculture sector, as mentioned by the director of an agriculture project, technology transfer is not possible without the government because NGOs may have less staff with specialised knowledge, and government officials in these sectors hold professional degrees and work experience in relevant fields. Not only are the requirements of professional and technical expertise applicable for GOs in engaging beneficiaries in the service sectors, but GOs' expertise is also beneficial for the training conducted by NGOs. GOs also have more advantages than NGOs in the specialised-service sectors, in which professional and technical expertise are required to engage beneficiaries. For example, farmers obtain technical knowhow from the DAE field staff when the training is organised by NGOs. When it is a matter of providing training on health issues, NGOs organise it under project activities and invite public-sector health professionals to deliver specialised training to beneficiaries.

However, the specialised and technical skills that interviewees claimed to have come more from GOs are related to the capacity development of beneficiaries in the service sectors. GOs fulfil a single component of the BE process in the service sector. This finding is critical to determining whether technical expertise is sufficient for engaging beneficiaries. Hoyle (1990, 164) argues that technical knowledge and skills in the service sectors represent a limited context of engagement, and the wider context involves addressing engagement beyond technical expertise, including the social and economic aspects of development. In contrast, skills that interviewees mentioned regarding NGOs are related to engaging project beneficiaries, which covers a wide range of BE processes inclusive of human-rights-based approaches. These are NGO skills specific to BE in addition to building the beneficiary capacity in service sectors provided by GOs.

Scope of BE in GO–NGO training

Bangladesh has a strong institutional capacity to provide training to government officials, NGOs, the private sector and project beneficiaries. While NGOs are said to be more exposed to BE and participatory approaches to training, examining the courses of public-sector training institutions reveals how GOs, including UPs, are exposed to the concepts of

BE in the development field. Appendix D[31] provides a snapshot of basic-training content in the public-sector training institutions. These include the Bangladesh Public Administration Training Centre (BPATC), the National Academy of Planning and Development (NAPD), the Bangladesh Academy for Rural Development (BARD), the Rural Development Academy (RDA) and the National Institute of Local Government (NILG).

Given the wide range of courses that focus on public-sector management, development planning and project management at BPATC and NAPD, it cannot be identified whether BE has been one of the project-management tools. Training courses for core public service focus on delivering services to citizens as the fundamental responsibility of civil servants rather than developing concepts of integrating people into development. A senior civil servant who had worked in training institutions revealed in an interview that BE is not included as a topic in training courses. Capacity development is different in the public sector. There is no such module as development participation or BE in the public-sector training of key civil servants from entry level to senior staff. However, public-sector training courses do include poverty reduction and rural development. For hands-on experience in these development issues, trainees need to undertake field attachments, during which they conduct research studies on development interventions in specific rural locations. Training opportunities at BARD and RDA (including the BPATC trainee attachment at BARD and RDA) indicate that civil-service officials are exposed to rural development, entrepreneurship development, participatory approaches to development and capacity building of project beneficiaries. Training courses at BARD and RDA are offered to GOs, NGOs, project beneficiaries and people from the private sector. Therefore, public-service officials are familiar with and exposed to development participation and people orientation to development. However, the question is how many officials from public services and NGOs can attend these trainings. Apart from the core public servants, there are other government staff working at the field level recruited for development projects. Whether or not they are exposed to these training opportunities or receive on-the-job training to integrate beneficiaries for development participation cannot be confirmed. NGOs receive continuous training or take refresher courses, which may not be the reality for government staff working in the development field.

---

[31] A desk review was conducted during fieldwork on the training curriculums of different public-sector institutions, available on the websites of each (see Appendix D).

Scope of local-government training

The NILG, which is situated in Dhaka, is responsible for making the LGIs the centre of local-development activities through capacity development. The NILG provides training to local-government representatives and LGI officials on various issues, ranging from relevant laws, rules and regulations to local-level planning and development relevant to the various services that UPs provide. The training methods that NILG follows – such as group discussions, exchange of experiences, case studies, demonstrations and open discussions (NILG n. d.) – involve participatory approaches to capacity development. It also demonstrates how local-government training creates opportunities for UP representatives and officials to become exposed to the community-engagement aspect of local development. The public-sector training strategies in Bangladesh have been expanded to prepare LGIs so that they are familiar with the concept of participation in grassroots development activities.

NGO training and beneficiary engagement

As revealed in interviews and observed in secondary sources, participation, facilitation and team building are the major distinctive features of NGO training. Unlike public-sector training, which is centrally organised, NGO training is on-the-job and mostly provided at the local level for NGO fieldworkers. For example, the principles of BRAC training include needs based, participatory, results oriented, problem solving and experience based (BRAC Learning Division n. d.). Ahmed and Rafi (1999, 3) argue that learning and development are key features of BRAC, which is "constantly used in redefining the development strategies" and has been the mode of policy planning within the organisation. Training content is based on program needs, such as the Madaripur Legal Aid Association (MLAA) working on access to justice for marginalised people, and providing legal and human-rights training to fieldworkers on various legal issues relevant to core programs and projects (MLAA n. d.). Similarly, some short training courses that the Rangpur–Dinajpur Rural Service (RDRS) provides include facilitation-skill development, basic training on value-chain development, community-driven development, the promotion of entrepreneurship, group dynamics, leadership development and team building, and savings and microfinance management, which are designed for NGO staff and project beneficiaries (RDRS n. d.).

Training courses are relevant to the everyday functions of NGO staff who work with project beneficiaries. These NGO-led training activities, in terms of content and recipients, appear to be different from those of public-sector opportunities, as was identified in interviews. However, NGO training is designed for NGO staff, fieldworkers and development practitioners. While NGOs can participate in training courses offered by public-sector training institutes, as observed in BPATC (which offers short courses open to NGOs and private-sector employees), BARD and RDA courses, it is not evident in the primary or secondary data sources whether government officials take part in these NGO-led training opportunities. This indicates a possible knowledge gap between GOs and NGOs regarding BE, which places NGOs in an advantageous position.

NGO advantage of M&E skills

In attributing advantages to NGOs, M&E skills are considered an essential element of BE because they require continuous monitoring, and are better than those of their government counterparts. NGOs have the advantage of being able to monitor project activities on a regular basis through their staff presence at the grassroots level and interactions with beneficiaries. M&E is still a challenge in the public sector. The guidelines for NGOs are focused on beneficiary participation that enables NGO staff to engage project beneficiaries. For example, NGOs that are partnered with the PKSF need M&E professionals to monitor and report on the project progress. This clearly outlines monitoring procedures at two levels: the implementation process and the project results at the community level (PKSF n. d.). The M&E tools include baseline questionnaires, beneficiary profiles and community profiles, which would not be possible without engaging project beneficiaries.

NGO fieldworkers are based in the project area, which provides an added advantage for ensuring beneficiary engagement in the monitoring and evaluation. Being present in the field and having specialised M&E skills are required for reporting that is developed based on information from beneficiaries. An NGO executive mentioned that his NGO had an effective M&E tool, and that reports were developed on baseline data that staff gathered from interactions with beneficiaries. NGO reports on project implementation include beneficiary feedback, case studies and individual stories, which were identified in sample reports, as available on different NGO websites. The funding organisations, such as PKSF and GOs, monitor NGO-implemented projects. Moreover, NGOs need to ensure beneficiary integration in M&E documentation when donor funding is received. Donors have their own templates to comply with.

M&E in GOs

Strategies for transferring development policies into practises include local administration, decentralisation and enhancing UP capacity to engage communities in local development (as discussed in chapter two). Data obtained from primary and secondary sources demonstrated that the availability of staff at the field level creates opportunities for GOs to ensure interactions with beneficiaries, which is evident in agriculture development. While discussing M&E, one of the agriculture officials mentioned that they are present at the field level, where they are responsible for door-to-door visits. As per the demand of the farmers, they provide advice. “This is the main reason for the miracle advancement of the agriculture in Bangladesh,” as an agriculture officer and NGO executive said, also mentioning that this physical presence helps monitoring at the field level. However, the presence of government staff varies from department to department, which was revealed during an interview with a UH&FPO. There are vacant positions in the UPZ Health Complex, making BE challenging for this sector. Despite the scope of engaging beneficiaries in M&E, as mentioned in the government’s development planning, research participants expressed concerns about the required skills of the M&E process to engage beneficiaries in the public sector. One project staff member noted that in terms of project evaluation through beneficiary participation, it is important to observe how they receive the services; however, there are concerns over whether beneficiaries take part in evaluations in the absence of the required skills.

The challenge of M&E in the public sector has been reiterated throughout its development planning, as shown in Fig. 4.1. The government emphasised the need for improved M&E and project management, which has been detailed in the FYPs. The Internal Monitoring and Evaluation Department (IMED) was established to ensure M&E for project success. The FYPs underscore the need to ensure M&E for development in different sectors, so it has been incorporated to ensure the implementation of projects and deliver the benefits to citizens.

The first FYP integrated the evaluation of projects and considered quality assurance (GOB 1973). The fourth FYP directly linked M&E with beneficiaries (GOB 1995). The other FYPs recognised M&E as a success factor for the implementation of development projects. Apart from the FYPs, the IMED’s functions incorporate field inspections to oversee project-implementation status, identification of implementation problems and recommending solutions for better project management. The M&E guidelines available on the IMED website (IMED n. d.) provided a template for officials who were responsible for onsite project inspection and outlined the pre-inspection and inspection requirements. Sections 8.9 and 16 of the

Fig. 4.1. M&E in the government's development planning

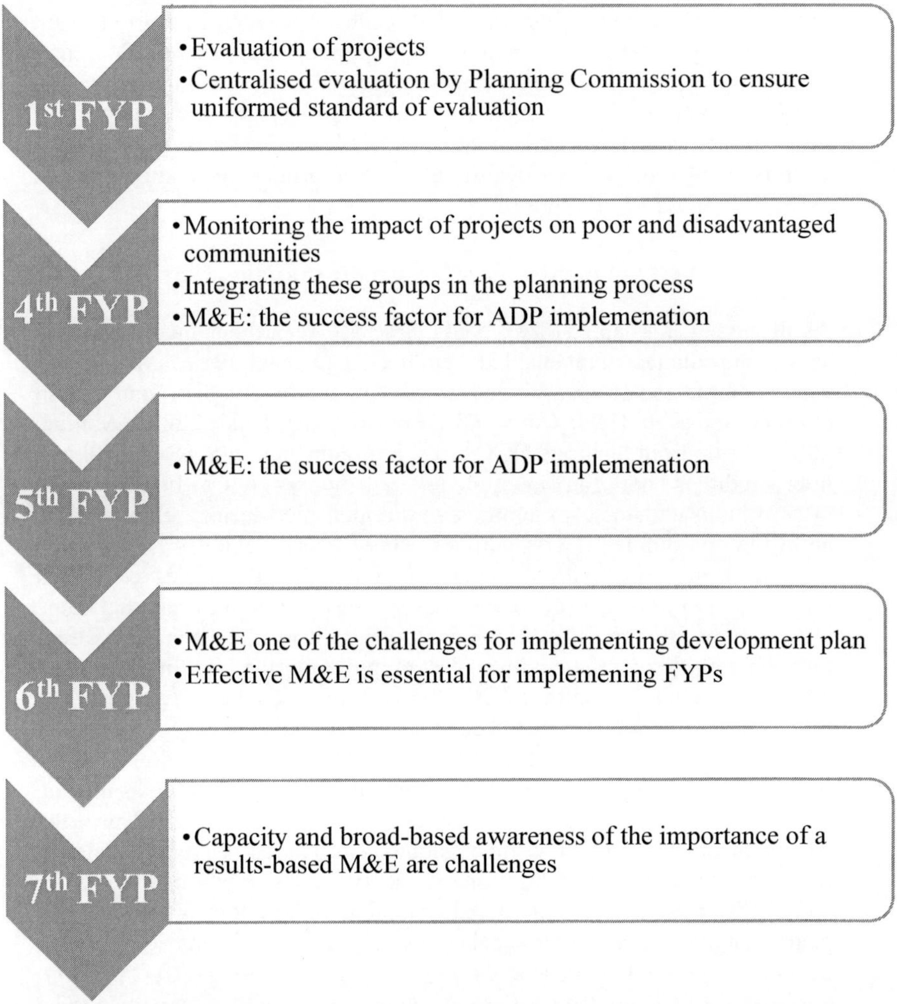

Source: Dutta (2021a)

guidelines advised the provision of inspection reports following discussions with project target populations. In an updated 2004 version, the template requires opinions from project beneficiaries for general observations on the project. A few M&E reports available from government websites include the Maternal, Child, Reproductive and Adolescent Health project, the

Women Computer Training project and the Primary Education Development Program (IMED n. d.). The reports do not detail interactions with beneficiaries, but some general comments imply that feedback was obtained from them. For example, it was mentioned in the report on the Women Computer Training project that women trainees suggested having a training manual would be beneficial. However, how much projects have benefitted the beneficiaries, and whether beneficiaries provided feedback on access to maternal and reproductive health services or primary education are not outlined in these M&E reports.

NGO expertise in microcredit management

As discussed in chapter three, NGO expertise regarding microcredit and small-loans management enabled them to engage beneficiaries. Microcredit is one of the major areas in which NGOs are involved in Bangladesh (Ahmed and Rafi 1999; Cons and Paprocki 2010; Haider 2011; Mallick 2002). Aside from the large NGOs such as Grameen Bank, ASA or BRAC, microcredit is now an integral part of many NGOs linking these organisations with the communities, as was identified during fieldwork. The ability to communicate with individual beneficiaries enables NGOs to be successful in microcredit management and gain advantages of BE in comparison to GOs. One of the NGO executives interviewed said that if one project ends, BE activities also end. However, it is evident in many areas that beneficiaries continue with project outputs after three or four years of a project's lifetime because of BE through microcredit provisions. The research participants from NGOs interviewed were mostly working in microcredit management either as a partner organisation to the PKSF or with funds from donors for the implementation of projects, such as income generation or the development of ethnic-minority group projects. This is the advantage attributed to NGOs in engaging beneficiaries. Given that interest recovery for NGOs starts after one week, BE is a continuous process for NGOs. Their expertise in microcredit, small grants and loan management is instrumental for engaging project beneficiaries at the individual level, which connects NGOs to the households, as Islam and Walkerden (2015) identify. Research participants from GOs and NGOs considered this expertise to be an advantage of NGOs in engaging beneficiaries in the development context of Bangladesh.

Outreach to Project Beneficiaries

Public outreach is important for engaging project beneficiaries, and it involves going door-to-door in project settings. This ability of NGOs to reach out to communities has made them more effective in this respect. NGO project staff visit the households of target beneficiaries on a regular basis. This begins during the project design and continues throughout the project cycle. Going to individual households shapes the NGO project design as required data for social mapping come directly from beneficiaries. It is important for NGOs to conduct social mapping to identify what resources there are and what is required to link projects with government-development initiatives. Door-to-door visits and social mapping enable NGOs to survey the area in detail and consider local needs, beliefs, values and attitudes (Sarker 2005, 260). Islam and Walkerden (2015, 1708) argue that there should be adequate "bonding" and "bridging" to build community and social networks, which require institutional support. NGOs are institutions that can establish "social networks," which is important for engaging communities. NGOs can reach target beneficiaries through courtyard meetings, and inform people about development and projects because of their reach to beneficiaries. The discussion that started in the 1990s on NGO's connection with beneficiaries has continued in the development context of Bangladesh. Outreach to beneficiaries is one of the success factors of family-planning projects, as revealed during interviews. NGOs worked very well in the fields of maternal health and family planning involving beneficiaries, which could be test cases for NGO success in project implementation and BE, as indicated by research participants.

The same aspect of reaching beneficiaries has been revealed in interviews with FWVs at the union health centre. They felt the benefits of having NGO fieldworkers in family-planning projects to reach beneficiaries for a wide coverage, as it is otherwise difficult for FWVs to cover all areas. It is important to note that BE in the health sector is not only about family-welfare services and the family-planning program, but also covers a wide range of objectives and activities in the sector-wide program for the overall improvement of the health, population and nutrition sub-sectors (MoHFW n. d.). Therefore, having skilled fieldworkers for each of the sub-sectors is critical for GOs to engage beneficiaries. In reviewing the nature and extent of community participation in the family-planning program of five countries, including Bangladesh, Askew and Khan (1990, 131) argue that community-based service provisions are dependent on full-time individuals who provide services at the community level, such as the FWVs in Bangladesh. Direct contact with beneficiaries is important for GOs or NGOs in project management and having staff to talk to them is something that beneficiaries value. Direct interactions connect people with development activities irrespective of which organisation is implementing the projects. GOs can reach beneficiaries when project staff or department officials are based in the field with the specific function of connecting beneficiaries, such as the DAE, the UPZ health office or the UPs. These findings reiterate the importance of having staff to transfer the policies of BE into practice at the field level, which is also evident in many public-sector projects that reach beneficiaries at the union level.

Engaging women beneficiaries

Engaging women beneficiaries is sometimes difficult for GOs, and NGOs are of significant help in this issue. Interviews revealed that, with assistance from NGOs, it was easier for the DAE to ensure women's participation in training and crop-production demonstration programs. This is because NGOs have more women staff than GOs at the grassroots level. It is important to note that no female Upazila or union-level officials were seen while conducting interviews with DAE officials. One of the NGO executives interviewed mentioned that the NGO had 220 field staff, of which 70 were women who have portfolios because most of the work is with women beneficiaries. In the fields of health and family welfare, the FWVs interviewed were women who interact with other women in households in rural areas, which enhances their participation in public-health awareness programs. However, not all service sectors within the government have adequate numbers of female staff at the union levels; for example, how many union-agriculture officials are women could be the subject of a separate investigation. Therefore, there is a need for not only staff in the field but also ensuring the presence of women staff, which makes it easier to engage women beneficiaries, and thus the advantage is attributed to NGOs. However, the public sector is rolling out projects at the union level to connect women beneficiaries. For example, the Totthoapa project under MoWCA is rolled out in each UP, through which women beneficiaries receive information related to various services like agriculture, health, education, legal assistance and entrepreneurship. Here, decentralised information portals at the field level connect women beneficiaries to different services (MoWCA n. d.).

UP to connect communities

Research participants mentioned that having service delivery provisions at the UP is more advantageous for the government in engaging project beneficiaries. Provisions in UP functions facilitate these organisations to bring communities closer to local development. When UPs are the implementing partners for projects, it becomes easier for NGOs to engage communities. This appears to be obvious in Bangladesh in a project like Activating Village Courts[32], under which village-court infrastructure and service provisions were developed in selected UPs. Interviews with the project staff revealed that having UP as the host organisation of this project at the grassroots level enabled NGOs to access beneficiaries without resistance because the local community is more familiar to UP members.

Engaging beneficiaries in difficult-to-reach areas

Engaging communities in difficult-to-reach areas is another advantageous area for NGOs in comparison to GOs. Despite GOs' countrywide administrative networks, geographical locations and UPs in each of the unions, there are regions in Bangladesh where logistical support is inadequate for GOs to deliver services at the grassroots level. In addition, it requires understanding the diversity in the communities. This factor appears to be more applicable in regions where the country has tribal populations, for example the Chittagong Hill Tracts (CHT). An interview with a former project staff member with experience of working in this region revealed that, due to its geographical location and ethnocultural differences, the long-term placement of government staff was a difficulty. For this reason, local NGOs have more advantages for engaging project beneficiaries.

The role of GOs in integrating people in remote regions with the national development is more persuasive at the national level. For example, the government undertakes projects to promote development in CHT, in which communities of ethnic and cultural diversity are spread over twenty-five UPZs in mountainous areas. In this context, policies and project-implementation strategies require significant considerations for engaging beneficiaries and delivering services in these remote areas. In such a context, local NGOs were preferred for engaging communities.

---

[32] An EU funded project jointly implemented by the LGRD and UNDP Bangladesh. More information is available at
https://www.eeas.europa.eu/delegations/bangladesh/activating-village-courts-bangladesh-%E2%80%93-phase-ii-avcb-ii_en?s=164

Authority to Engage Project Beneficiaries

In identifying the advantages of GOs and NGOs, research participants discussed beneficiary perceptions of and attitudes towards these organisations that impact their participation in the development process. As revealed in interviews, engagement needs to build beneficiary confidence, which is a prerequisite for their being involved in project activities or development initiatives. Research participants mentioned that the presence of GOs enhances that confidence. There were several factors why research participants thought the authority of GOs made it easier for NGOs to engage beneficiaries.

Enhancing the confidence of beneficiaries

Beneficiaries can be sceptical about new initiatives, or if they see that new initiatives are affecting their daily life. That is why communicating development benefits, as discussed in the previous chapter, is instrumental to engaging beneficiaries. The reasons identified in interviews include the authority of GOs, beneficiary's scepticism regarding new initiatives and opportunities to raise concerns to the higher levels of GOs. These factors make initiatives more acceptable to beneficiaries as they have "aastha" (reliance, confidence or trust) in GOs. Their scepticism is intensified if they observe only NGOs or private companies advocating for development activities. BE does not depend on what the project intends to deliver or what methods NGOs or GOs follow; it depends on how beneficiaries perceive the project or services, or what benefits they will receive from them. If it is a matter of introducing a new variety of crops, maintaining health and sanitation or encouraging beneficiaries on social issues, convincing them seems to be a prerequisite for their participation.

This task of convincing becomes easier in the presence of GOs, though government staff also find it difficult to convince project beneficiaries to adapt to new technologies or services. According to a DAE official, "the great task is to convince the farmers." "Self-interest" is an important factor for beneficiary involvement in project activities (Purvis, Zagenczyk and McCray 2015). For service delivery, beneficiaries need to understand and observe the tangible benefits from their participation in any new development intervention. According to Oakley et al. (1991, 28–9), farmers tend to participate in such projects if the "actual benefit is tied with participation." The benefits need to be "obvious and tangible," and demonstrations and trials are effective for beneficiary participation in these scenarios. As identified in interviews, engagement is not guaranteed unless beneficiaries can see the tangible outcome where neither GOs nor NGOs can impose anything. An additional finding is that understanding benefits also requires the presence of GOs, as revealed in an interview with the UH&FPO.

Research participants believed that GOs enhance trust because accountability to people ultimately lies with the government, which is the owner of development. NGOs may disappear but the public sector remains, no matter what form of government the country has. Therefore, the responsibility of enhancing beneficiary confidence lies with GOs and not NGOs. This finding is related to the administrative context of Bangladesh and its gradual development of the administrative system. According to Zafarullah (2007, 166), bureaucracy in Bangladesh obtained "acceptability and stability in the society," and frequent changes in political regimes and leadership "unwittingly compelled the people to rely on the more 'durable' bureaucracy."

Enforceability: a tool for BE?

In the Bangladesh context, NGOs are perceived as the implementing partners to GOs, and that the authority to implement development programs remains with GOs. Enforceability is perceived as an engagement tool. The decision-making authority of GOs makes it easier for NGOs to engage project beneficiaries. In distinguishing public organisations from the non-public sector within the discussion of organisational theories, Gortner, Nichols and Ball (2007, 3–4) argue that organisational structures influence functions, and that both structures and functions are critical for achieving goals. The bureaucratic structure of the government is usually thought to be less effective in comparison to NGOs, which are perceived as being flexible. However, enforceability in the development field provides GOs with authority, which is important as beneficiaries can rely on it rather than accepting the assumed flexibility of NGOs in the development context of Bangladesh. The authority of GOs through administrative networks at the field level is often helpful for mobilising project beneficiaries because, when invited by a deputy commissioner[33] or Upazila Nirbahi Officer (UNO),[34] citizens cannot refuse to come to the event or join the consultation. This is because "public oversight and accountability are prominent and necessary features" of governments, which were "created by law to administer law" (Gortner, Nichols and Ball 2007, 5). However, while NGOs

---

[33] Administrative head of the district administration. Sixty-four districts are headed by the same number of Deputy Commissioners.

[34] Head of the sub-district administration.

take advantage of GOs' authority to obtain beneficiary consent for coming to the event, it cannot be claimed that beneficiaries are engaged in disseminating their opinions or are able to decide in the development process. GOs' authority is an administrative or procedural requirement for NGOs to involve people in the development process instead of engaging them. However, in relating authority to BE, research participants felt that the authority of GOs is perceived as positive when it is used and shared in partnership with the development objective of NGOs, and allows beneficiaries to participate.

NGOs engage beneficiaries as agreed by GOs

NGOs are responsible for implementing projects agreed by GOs or donors or approved by GOs. It is the government counterpart who lays out conditions and guidelines on how to engage beneficiaries, such as guidelines for FWVs in health projects or diaries for union-agriculture officers in agriculture projects. When NGOs are responsible for implementing the same government, donor-funded or NGO-funded projects in these sectors, they also follow the same guidelines. NGOs do not have much scope to introduce anything new as projects are sometimes implemented in sensitive areas, and BE needs to be aligned to government guidelines, as identified by an NGO executive. It is obvious that BE needs to follow guidelines that are applicable for both GOs and NGOs in its process. Reaching beneficiaries becomes easier for NGOs if they have agreements from GOs, or if GOs, as implementing agencies, have permission from the top. BE becomes easier for NGOs when formal agreement is obtained from GOs. For example, a letter works as a safeguard, which was noted by a project-management staff member saying "government officials at the field level depend on high-up's orders to obtain beneficiary participation. NGOs try to generate office orders [from the ministry] and are then able to engage beneficiaries."

The authority of the GOs appears to be inevitable for engaging beneficiaries; however, the objective is more like facilitating BE activities within the boundaries of GOs' agreements. This is a functional aspect of BE which NGOs cannot exercise, and therefore depend on GOs to reach beneficiaries and coordinate with other agencies to implement projects. For example, NGOs implementing the Village Courts project had to work with UPs that are under the Ministry of Local Government and Rural Development (LGRD), and office orders from the ministry helped NGOs and the project management to coordinate with UPs and engage beneficiaries, as identified by a project-management staff member. To this end, the authority of GOs is advantageous for NGOs in engaging project beneficiaries.

The scope of BE for NGOs appears to be limited or difficult in the absence of GOs.

Leading committees connect beneficiaries

GOs lead various project-management committees from central to union levels, which results in decision making in consultation with implementing partners, leading interviewees to believe that GOs have more advantages over NGOs in this. Apart from project committees at the national level, officials from the field administration lead GO–NGO coordination committees at the local level, in which NGOs report to the GOs in monthly meetings on project progress and development activities implemented by NGOs. For example, the UNO is the head of the UPZ Coordination Committee. At the UP level, development committees are headed by the UP chairperson. According to research participants, the representation of GOs in various committees reassured NGO access to beneficiaries. These committees, mainly at the union level, included NGOs and representatives from local communities that enabled beneficiaries to interact with GOs, NGOs and the project team. For example, government officials join these village committees in CHT projects and interact directly with beneficiaries. Communities also benefit from the presence of GOs because they can talk directly to them through these village committees.

NGO Advocacy and BE

While the GOs' presence matters for convincing project beneficiaries and obtaining their confidence for their participation, NGO advocacy also plays a significant role in mobilising them. The NGO role of advocacy is considered as a critical factor for beneficiary engagement, which is seldom attributed to GOs in the existing literature. In analysing practises in Bangladesh on NGO roles in development and democracy, Rahman (2006) identified political tensions of NGO advocacy when the parties in power perceive this advocacy to be politically driven or patronised by the opposition party. The author argue that, despite this perception, NGOs hold "considerable room" for social mobilisation and advocacy programs, through which NGOs like BRAC and Nijera Kori proved their potential (467). Research participants identified that NGOs' advocacy role had multiple dimensions for BE, ranging from advocacy events and sharing information to individually conveying project purposes to beneficiaries.

Project launching and information sharing

It is important to inform people about projects, and NGOs organise project launch events that have more public outreach than GOs can achieve. Information sharing on projects is the gateway to engaging beneficiaries, which is conducted in a more formal and professional way. The presence of GOs is an important factor for NGOs' information sharing; however, NGO expertise in organising such events is essential for conducting project advocacy, and NGOs provide information received from beneficiaries to GOs, this advocacy helping GOs to make informed decisions. Project launching is an important event for communicating the project objectives to the target beneficiaries. Officials from government departments, UP and different stakeholders help to communicate project purposes, following which NGO fieldworkers go to beneficiaries and form beneficiary groups, which is followed by awareness raising. NGOs conduct advocacy for awareness raising and this also helps policymaking. The best example, as revealed in FGD of NGOs, is the case of the Thakurgaon district hospital that initiated a special counter for Dalit people, led by the government based on NGO advocacy.

Although the presence of GOs is crucial for beneficiaries to participate in such events, the ability of NGOs to reach individual beneficiaries is helpful in mobilising people to participate in GO-led advocacy events, such as health-awareness programs or observing a national day. The UH&FPO in his interview mentioned that NGOs liaise with the UPZ Health Complex to provide support for these government events, and there is no problem with GOs allowing them to do so.

Engaging requires going beyond advocacy

Individual interaction with beneficiaries is important for beneficiary engagement and NGOs appear to be in a more advantageous position than GOs. It is important to determine whether GOs have any flexibility in undertaking extra efforts that are beyond the project provisions or fall outside the project activities required for BE.[35] Jamil (2002, 110) notes that bureaucrats in Bangladesh are overly concerned with rules, and there is not "enough flexibility and room to adjust goals and procedures." An interesting practical experience was noted during an interview with a project-management staff member, formerly a civil servant. Although his experience was more than

[35] As evident in the NGO experience of mobilising training participation, mentioned in Box 2.

a decade earlier, it showed that being flexible and going beyond traditional roles may not always be an acceptable attitude in a bureaucratic environment. As a UNO, he once tried to sit in the local tea stall to talk to people and gain insights on various local issues, but was highly discouraged from doing so by his senior colleagues. Having the administrative networks and infrastructure of GOs present in remote rural areas may not be adequate or logistically convenient for reaching beneficiaries, mainly when engagement activities need to be implemented. Activities are not simply inviting beneficiaries to workshops or stakeholder consultations but involve different methods and techniques to engage them. The local base in the community, flexibility and access to individual beneficiaries help NGOs utilise different techniques for engaging communities.

Engaging Within GO–NGO Limitations

The above discussions highlight the advantages of both GOs and NGOs that enable these organisations to engage beneficiaries within project settings. Both these organisations equally experience limitations that make BE difficult in the country's development context. The inclusion of beneficiaries is limited for NGOs, given that their functions are limited to certain projects and project areas. There are associated costs that GOs and NGOs need to implement for BE activities, and the selection of committee members, processes for engaging and perceptions of BE are sometimes challenging for them. Above all, beneficiary choices factor in engaging that ultimately lead to their participation in the development process. The following sections illustrate these limitations in detail.

Inclusion is limited for NGOs

GOs can ensure the inclusion of wider communities as policies do not limit focusing on any target groups, which is a reality for NGOs. When it is a matter of engaging large-scale beneficiaries beyond projects, GOs have more advantages as NGOs need to implement projects and engage beneficiaries, as stated in the project documents, and are limited to the target populations. In contrast, GOs implement development activities for beneficiaries across all administrative units[36] as it is more convenient for them to do so. This is mainly evident where NGOs do not have good coverage and therefore a limited presence.

---

[36] See the section on administrative units in Table 1.1.

BRAC is an implementing partner for managing the microcredit component of an agricultural-development project. Therefore, engaging beneficiaries in the specific area is limited to those who receive loans. Likewise, NGOs are limited in the health sector as they do not have wide coverage and are the implementing partners of health projects. For example, the government funding for the tuberculosis program was disbursed to NGOs like BRAC to carry out development programs. According to a senior official in the Directorate of Health and the UH&FPO, the NGO role is to assist government health agencies and provide logistical support to government activities on health issues. They perceived that NGO roles are now limited and these organisations must seek permission from the directorate to start work.

These findings are critical for examining the extent of BE in the health sector. The previous section analysed data from interviews with FWVs who experienced difficulties in reaching out to all people in the community because NGOs are not much involved in this area nowadays. Therefore, considering NGOs to be providers of logistical services to health programs shows that GOs' perceptions of NGO roles in BE are limited to logistical support. However, these findings do not confirm that NGOs are not required for BE in the health sector. Rather, the data indicates individual perceptions about NGO contributions that restrict their activities to the implementation of project components or providing logistic support to the government organising events for beneficiaries.

The cost of BE

GOs perceive that management costs related to BE for NGOs are higher than for GOs. The events and programs that NGOs undertake to engage beneficiaries require more resources for arranging big events. More importantly, resources are critical for delivering project benefits. Government funds, foreign-development assistance and internal resources enable NGOs to plan, formulate, implement and evaluate projects. At the same time, obtaining individual skills and the ability to engage beneficiaries are essential for delivering the project benefits. However, the cost is not only associated with NGOs' management. The process of BE to ensure their participation is a resource-intensive task, which was described by an NGO executive. There is a cost of participation if events or ways of participation are to be meaningful. When beneficiaries are mobilised for an event, it has a "negative impact" on their daily wages. NGOs need to subsidise or compensate this negative impact as beneficiaries will not participate without an incentive. Opportunity costs and time are associated with this engagement process: the return should be bigger than the beneficiary's daily wage. In addition, there might be a mismatch between demand and supply. The interview with the NGO executive revealed that when beneficiaries are engaged, the expectation wish list quickly grows and it is not possible to achieve all of it. Engagement is focused on supply and it becomes tricky at that point. NGOs subsidise or compensate for the negative impact as beneficiaries will not participate without compensation for what they lose. Opportunity costs and time are associated with this engagement process.

The question is whether this is different if carried out by the government. An important finding in this respect is that although it costs NGOs to engage beneficiaries, this is equally true for GOs because they not only have to pay incentives to beneficiaries but officials also require incentives, such as honoraria for their participation in events or consultation meetings. This finding brings out a critical aspect of not only costs associated with BE but also expenses in terms of honoraria or conveyances for GOs or other stakeholders participating in engagement events organised for beneficiaries.

Selection of committee members and beneficiaries

Representation in committees creates opportunities for communities to participate in development activities. However, primary-data sources identified that this approach is not easy at the UPZ level, where the government nominates committee members, as indicated by an NGO executive. Moreover, it also risks the politicisation that can divide marginalised groups, which was identified in an interview with a government official. In the recent past, NGO workers experienced challenges in accessing UPs, as noted in another interview. The NGO fieldworker clearly mentioned that it was challenging in the past when the UP chairperson and officials did not accept NGOs. The UPs even wanted to influence the volunteer selection, and "NGOs were not respected and had no access to UPs." This makes it challenging even for GOs to engage project beneficiaries. Research participants from a government directorate described beneficiary selection in the past as being a challenge when they experienced political pressure. UP chairpersons and members used to mobilise beneficiaries under the VGD[37] program to ensure their votes during UP elections.

[37] One of the social safety-net programs assisted by the World Food Program. Implemented by the Food Planning and Monitoring Unit under the Ministry of Food. See www.fpmu.gov.bd.

Process Versus People Orientation to BE

Given the bureaucratic nature of government functions evident in theories, GOs are more process-oriented whereas NGOs are people-oriented because they learn from people. Interestingly this was mentioned by a government respondent during the fieldwork. Government officials have transferable jobs, which causes frequent changes to project staff, such as the position of project director (PD). Moreover, if BE or people orientation is not a criterion for future promotion or opportunities, government officials might not consider their placement in projects as being important for their career path. The system of administrative procedures affects approaches to work in projects. There is a need to recognise project-management roles at the government's end to ensure BE. Unless it is recognised, PDs are also not keen to remain in the position as it deprives them of many other benefits of working in the mainstream ministries or departments. One government official regretted saying that if anything goes wrong, PDs are the ones responsible, and there is no team approach to understanding what caused the problem. The question is why a PD should risk engaging beneficiaries if it is not required in the project or promotion policy.

Administrative procedures must be convenient for implementing partners to ensure BE. The study identified how a memo from a government office makes it easier for NGOs to carry out BE. However, if there is no initiative of providing letters or formal concurrence, engagement activities are delayed. For example, a journalist working in a donor-funded project on creating young journalists (children above 10 years) revealed that he was coordinating with the district education officer to forward a letter to all schools to engage children in a media-reporting workshop. This was discussed in the district coordination meeting but not actually actioned as it was outside the district administration's routine work. This bureaucratic procedure might affect how GOs engage beneficiaries. An interview with an NGO official revealed that GOs invite beneficiaries or the UP chairperson to a big forum. There are doubts whether beneficiaries are engaged in such hierarchical and bureaucratic events. The above data confirm the findings from FGDs as displayed in Figs. 2.3 and 2.4, where research participants from GOs and NGOs aligned BE to process and people, respectively.

Pro-people Policies Versus Pro-people Implementation

Primary-data sources demonstrate that a positive and pro-people outlook is important for ensuring BE. Interviewees identified GOs' outlook on this as being a shortcoming to some extent. The history of bureaucratic culture has a "colonial legacy," which does not align with the government's pro-people policies. BE is a kind of relationship building that was identified by research participants. Engagement is providing information and obtaining feedback through regular interaction and monitoring. In a bureaucratic environment that originated in the colonial era, this quest for information or "search behaviour"[38] is limited by the boundary of organisation (Jamil 2002, 96). When engaging project beneficiaries requires building community relationships and day-to-day interactions, this limited "search behaviour" may make the engagement process difficult for GOs.

The influence of colonial legacies in administrative culture still provides obstacles for integrating people in development as it is a limitation for GOs becoming people-oriented, which has been known for some time. Following independence in 1971, the aspiration was to make the administration appropriate for the new state through a political commitment, and "concerns for rural development became a dominant" development agenda in the following years (Hakim 1987, 7, 279). This realisation might have impacts on pro-people policies because the government remains responsible for policy formulation that addresses the political mandates and makes GOs responsible for implementation. In addition to pro-people policies, pro-people implementation processes are equally critical for BE, for which NGOs are better placed than GOs. An interview with a project staff member noted that the government setup is a "fusion of the colonial regime and the war of independence." On one hand, the historical background of the colonial era influences government attitudes towards people, which is reflected in the policy-implementation approaches in many government offices. On the other, the war of independence gave the nation a mandate of pro-people development, which is illustrated in the Constitution and development planning. It is a huge struggle to change this attitude and remove the colonial influence, as admitted by several research participants. Therefore, BE is difficult. Government policies are pro-people but the "implementation tools hold colonial influence," which can cause "malfunctioning of beneficiary engagement," as a research participant observed.

It has been argued that the administrative reform that encouraged pro-people policies resulted in an "increasing role of NGOs in community-development activities in many developing countries including Bangladesh" (Jamil 2002, 99). It is important to have engagement as a core implementation strategy. Another project staff member mentioned that NGOs have different

[38] This is a scientific term used in market analysis. Here, it implies an approach to exploring contexts and knowing beneficiaries.

approaches to engaging beneficiaries and have taken these as core principles, which is obviously different from how the government functions. The GOs' authority seems to be beneficial for NGOs engaging beneficiaries, as discussed earlier in this chapter. However, this becomes difficult for NGOs when combined with bureaucratic attitudes or colonial influence. One NGO approach is to link beneficiaries to government offices for information on the various services that GOs provide. When GOs are rigid in providing information, it becomes difficult for NGOs to engage beneficiaries.

When Beneficiary Choices Matter

Data also demonstrated that bureaucratic cultures or individual attitudes are not the only limitations for GOs or NGOs that can affect BE. Several interviewees noted that the attitudes of beneficiaries sometimes make it challenging for GOs and NGOs to ensure BE throughout project lifecycles and beyond. To some extent, it depends on how beneficiaries respond to this engagement, and whether being engaged is convenient for their personal and social aspects. For example, DWA officials believed it was sometimes challenging to get women to participate in training given that its duration might conflict with their household responsibilities. Rectifying this required the substantial involvement of the Department, which made contact with their families and organised courtyard meetings to make it convenient for women to join project activities or any event.

Similarly, it can be challenging for other service sectors in the government. For example, DAE officials felt that beneficiary attitudes made engagement challenging. Despite having the knowledge, skills and financial resources, beneficiaries often do not want to test or receive new things. Therefore, BE required the categorisation of groups depending on how beneficiaries acted on engagement. There are different types of beneficiaries, such as those who are motivated quickly, those who wait and see and then try, those who want to be involved after seeing others, and those who are lazy and never want to do anything. Even if strategies are in place, engagement may still be difficult for GOs or NGOs because individual attitudes to participation in development activities are subject to beneficiary orientations to development. People-centred development has been much discussed in the development literature; however, when it is a matter of development participation, it appears that strategies need to be in place to make people development-oriented.

Corruption: A Barrier to Public Engagement

Two research participants mentioned that BE can be hindered by corruption. As discussed above, BE requires the flow of financial resources (such as government grants) to the organisations to be transparent. For example, if UPs need to pay a percentage of their allocated grants to any organisations concerned, this makes it difficult for a UP to implement government-development projects, and hence a question about its role in engaging beneficiaries arises. One project-management staff member said that institutionalised corruption needs to end to make development participation happen. Though only a couple of interviewees identified corruption as a barrier for BE, it is important to add it as another dimension to the theories to revisit development participation. While beneficiary choices matter in making communicating benefits an essential component of BE for development participation, many other factors can exist that beneficiaries are not aware of or that influence their decision to participate, and may make them more vulnerable. It is important to note that "fault lines" (for example, corruption, exploitation and misinformation) exist in the development process in any country. If these fault lines are not addressed, they tend to deal with a development agenda (for example, poverty) but not its causes (Thomas 2014). Income-generation activities are key for engaging beneficiaries. This raises a question of whether income generation should be the only BE approach for participation that beneficiaries consider, or if BE approaches should also empower people to identify other causes of poverty, one of which could be corruption. Understanding only the development benefits may ignore these types of queries for wider participation.

This chapter has provided some important parameters that both GOs and NGOs experience for BE. Interestingly, these parameters are interconnected. Advantages and limitations are evident for both GOs and NGOs that make BE either convenient or challenging given the differing nature of projects and service sectors. While NGOs are perceived as more people-oriented or GOs as more process-oriented, there are no absolute advantages for one in comparison to the other. BE is incorporated in the public-sector development projects despite the limitations it experiences. However, limitations are also associated with beneficiary perceptions and attitudes, which affect BE by GOs and NGOs. Participation depends on how beneficiaries understand and respond to development benefits. Against this backdrop, development participation by default includes BE, but it cannot be said that BE will result in development participation. In view of these advantages and limitations, the next chapter discusses the scope of GO–NGO partnership to maximise BE for participation.

Chapter Five

Institutional Partnership: A Desired Condition

The partnering of GOs and NGOs in Bangladesh is inevitable, while the advantages and limitations for BE that each organisation experiences are interconnected. Partnering for BE is an obvious strategy as none of these organisations holds an absolute advantage over the other in the development field to connect beneficiaries with development. The country also hosts a significant number of NGOs, including those with national and international reputations which have been working in the development field for decades. In the global context, partnerships between GOs and NGOs are largely influenced by individual-country context and the extent to which governments exert control over their nongovernmental counterparts (Clark 2006; Batley 2011). Gortner, Nichols and Ball (2007, 64–5) explain how public-sector agents could be instrumental in developing relations with people and other agencies. From both theoretical and organisational standpoints, these entities operate in accordance with the widespread belief that the government and its agents should act lawfully. Thus, the government structures its functions based on given authorities within which NGOs and communities operate and behave (Gortner, Nichols and Ball 2007).

Makuwira (2014, 44) refers to the different models of developmental partnership based on context, such as government-dominant, NGO-dominant, dual dominance between GOs and NGOs, and collaborative partnership. If the government is non-responsive to people's participation in development, or if NGOs prefer working in isolation and donors favour nongovernment-based funding, this context will impact GO–NGO relations in any country. Depending on the context, this bond could be either competitive or conflicting, or characterised by "co-production," meaning the relationship is bound by collaboration, with NGOs operating within favourable government policies and participating in policy planning (Coston 1998). In a relationship built on "co-production" and "collaboration," both GOs and NGOs function as joint major actors coexisting as complementarities (the relationship is based on comparative advantages and mutual benefits).

Above all, this arrangement "demonstrates a win-win agreement" (Coston 1998, 371, 374). At the same time, the development literature condemns the power structure underlying GO–NGO relations, citing the former's control over the latter and the attitudes of public-sector officials towards NGO executives and staff as particularly oppressive (Ahmad 2002; Jamil 1998; Karim 1996; Sanyal 1991). NGO accountability towards beneficiaries in Bangladesh also receives many critiques given its inclination towards donors (Tarannum 2009; Islam 2016; TIB 2007). Whatever is written in the development literature, it is critical to identify the existing GO–NGO relationship in Bangladesh, or in other words how GOs and NGOs are working together to achieve participation in the country's development context. As such, this chapter aims to identify issues relating to the GO–NGO partnership which directly address BE in practice – given that the GO–NGO interdependence in terms of advantages and limitations in the development field requires understanding the existing relations that GOs and NGOs hold when attempting to connect with development recipients – and further reveal any opportunities to foster viable partnerships supporting BE that enhances development participation.

GO–NGO ties in the development field in Bangladesh are perceived at three levels. First, the partnership exists in the form of implementation, coordination and donor preference for development assistance. Second, the emergence of the private sector and role of UPs in development instigate NGOs to reinvigorate cross-sector relationships aimed at engaging beneficiaries. Finally, there are a few developmental issues that require close attention to improve GO–NGO bonds with each other and development beneficiaries. Based on the findings discussed in earlier chapters, this chapter is consequently divided into two sections. The first provides an analysis of how existing partnerships are currently addressing BE in the country's development initiatives. This is followed by an examination of the emerging opportunities that research participants deemed most appropriate for expanding GO–NGO relations.

Coordination as an Approach to BE

Research participants across different groups shared the view that coordination between GOs and NGOs is an inevitable and desired condition to and for BE. Given the noted advantages and limitations that both sides present (see chapter four), participants considered GO–NGO partnerships essential for enhancing public participation in national-development initiatives. For example, one respondent explained how a coordinated approach is expected for better beneficiary engagement (see Box 5), while another said that for both the GOs and NGOs, it is important to have the ability to work together.

Most research participants acknowledged that partnership exists in various forms when managing development projects. Notably, strategies on organisational coordination, agreements between GOs and NGOs, and enlisting nongovernment bodies as implementing partners in development projects are just some forms of how administrative collaboration takes place in Bangladesh. Interactions between GOs and NGOs generally occur at the organisational level, which research participants otherwise interpreted as coordination at different levels. That is, organisational interaction exists at the central level in Dhaka and expands to field administration at the district, UPZ and union levels. Participants wholly believed that coordination is and remains a mandatory task in government policy with which both GOs and NGOs must comply if to ensure BE.

Box 5. BE is difficult if not coordinated well

Coordination with the government does not seem to be a part of the project work plan (which is directly funded by a bilateral aid agency), so the project management does not need to coordinate with any government department. The project creates a value chain for mango growers, and project staff work directly with farmers who produce mangoes. As a part of the food-safety program, the government initiated the destruction of adulterated mangoes. In this approach to stopping food adulteration, a few project beneficiaries were affected, despite not having adulterated mangoes. Project beneficiaries lost their means of production and the creation of the value chain stalled. Eventually, the project had to contact district administration for a coordination meeting with other departments so that proper screening was in place and project beneficiaries were not affected. Coordination meetings were held and a campaign was launched jointly by government departments, NGOs and project managers that ensured the destruction of adulterated mangoes did not affect beneficiaries under the said project.

Coston (1998, 361–2) identified different types of GO–NGO relationships that can be characterised as either rivalry or competition, or complementarity or collaboration. This influences the extent of partnership between the two and further determines NGO links with GOs. Unlike these forms of connection, research participants in interviews identified "coordination" between GOs and NGOs as a contributing factor for BE, whereby interaction occurs to achieve development participation and addressing their requirements in the project implementation. Essentially, the GO–NGO partnership in the development context of Bangladesh is primarily driven by organisational coordination, as demonstrated in most respondents' answers. This GO–NGO coordination is based on "information sharing, resource sharing and joint actions," which are equally applicable to "cooperation," in line with definitions of different types of government and NGO partnership provided by Coston (1998, 370–1). Appendix E shows how research participants linked BE to coordination as a formal approach to interactions incorporated into the government function, as well as coordination procedures identified throughout discussions.

An approach to coordination, as indicated by research participants, seems to represent formal interaction between GOs and NGOs, mainly conducted through monthly and quarterly meetings at the district and UPZ levels, with development coordination meetings at the union level, and through NGOs reporting to government bodies on project progress. Importantly, NGO activities are reviewed in coordination meetings, which are usually chaired by the government department heads (e.g. the UNO in the UPZ Development Coordination Committee). At the central level, coordination meetings involve project-management groups, donors (if foreign-funded) and implementing agencies, including NGOs. At the UPZ and district levels, government agencies are responsible for holding NGO coordination meetings. There are also quarterly UPZ coordination meetings with NGOs chaired by the UNO, and ones held at the local level where interaction involves GO, NGOs and the UP. Importantly, the UP chairperson, the UNO and UP members conduct these meetings where NGOs implement projects in rural areas. Essentially, regular consultation ensures that institutional interactions occur between government officials of different service-sector departments in each UPZ and between GOs and NGOs.

Coordination meetings serve two purposes. Although they house the accomplishments of routine departmental work, they also facilitate the monitoring of project implementation. However, this interactive approach is less effective for BE if project initiatives are not formally coordinated between GOs, project units and the implementing agencies (such as NGOs) involved. While interviewing an evaluation officer of a fully foreign-funded project, it was found that lack of coordination certainly affects engagement efforts in development projects and further complicates the ability of staff to implement various components of a project (see Box 5) and affects development participation. Essentially, NGO activities are reviewed in these coordination meetings for potential overlaps, and government officials provide suggestions and further observe the progress of NGO-run events. Interaction between GOs and NGOs also happens through monthly, quarterly and annual progress reports. However, direct interaction with beneficiaries is limited in this. It is expected that reportage on project progress is instead based on beneficiary requirements obtained through interactions and the social mapping of beneficiaries that NGOs usually conduct for project planning.

That said, coordination is not solely limited to meetings. Rather, it accumulates through regular contact between GOs and NGOs to address issues of engagement and service delivery. An NGO fieldworker revealed that the government is one of the major stakeholders with which the NGO works. The NGO coordinates with the UPZ Education Office so there is regular communication with schools on vulnerable students having access to education, equal rights and access to the basic services the schools provide in the project area. The NGO conveys beneficiary requirements to the government through the UPZ Education Office. Every year, the NGO receives books and distributes them among students in schools. In addition, NGO reports help government departments reporting on local development. For example, the NGO provides reports to the livestock department, which uses the coverage in the government reporting on the overall livestock status in the local area (such as at the district level). NGOs have visual statistics of the development that it provides GOs and that contribute to the government's reporting system. This represents the informal coordination that takes place beyond scheduled meetings, such as visiting departments and talking to officials. This kind of interaction is directly related to BE: that is, an NGO will receive feedback and knowledge directly from beneficiaries and convey that information to GOs; in return, this enables NGOs to provide services to the people and placate their needs. Interviews also revealed that GO–NGO coordination in reporting not only aids government reportage but also influences its communication with UN bodies and in different international forums. This is exactly why NGO involvement in government programs is necessary – so that development reporting is based solely on information gathered at the local level involving beneficiaries.

GO–NGO Partnership: A Formal and Complementary Approach to BE

The GO–NGO partnership is established in the form of defining the role of NGOs in project agreements – between either GOs and NGOs, or GOs and donors – which involve NGOs in the project implementation. In this approach, the partnership continues as is agreed in the development-cooperation agreements established between donor agencies and GOs. It was noted that, in the agreement between the ERD (representing the GOs), donors define how best to involve NGOs. Essentially, this depends on what type of projects are undertaken and whether NGOs are to be engaged or not.

It is important to note that projects must be centred on recipients to properly define the nature of the GO–NGO partnerships in the corresponding agreements. Thus, cooperation (from an engagement perspective) seems to be a preconditioned and guided strategy of either the government or donors, as discussed earlier. Under such agreements, NGOs function as implementing partners to GOs, where trust is based on contractual pacts that dictate project management, as agreed upon by the government or respective donor involved. For example, one non-profit organisation is responsible for developing reading habits under the Secondary Education project, as selected through a bidding process. Conversely, when projects are donor-funded, agreement between the donors and governments decides if NGOs are to be selected as implementing partners. Alam (2011) cited that donor preference, terms and conditions have also been considered as enabling factors in said partnerships, evidenced in ADB-funded urban-health projects across Bangladesh. It is again required under formal agreement and government provisions that NGOs are chosen and made responsible for BE efforts.

This approach to partnership is reflected in project documents that authorise NGOs to formally engage development beneficiaries. Here, Alam (2011, 275–7) identifies that government conditions and donor preferences shape GO–NGO relations when delivering development outcomes, whereby GOs maintain relations with NGOs through the terms and conditions outlined in a "pre-fixed contract paper." Evidently, interviews with respondents highlighted that, under contracts, provisions of developmental partnership evolve around service delivery that incorporates BE. For example, public health and family welfare, education, training, microcredit management, awareness and advocacy, and capacity building for income generation all gain their advantages from NGO practises (see chapter three).

Despite contractual obligations, it is a desired condition that both GOs and NGOs engage in non-confrontational and cooperative relations. Government bodies seem to welcome collaborative strategies in partnerships with NGOs for managing development interventions. This notion was reflected in participants' responses, which did not emphasise any institutional or policy barriers that hinder the development of such ties. For example, one respondent noted how the government has public-private partnerships and collaborations with other agencies, as national-development policy allows NGOs to partner with government institutions. Similarly, another saw no problem in these complementary partnerships because the government also agrees to receive support from NGOs, which is required for transferring BE policy into practice (discussed in chapter two). However, from a nongovernment perspective, this bond might be convenient if focused on BE for development participation. That is, the government is the main stakeholder of development. The support it receives from NGOs is like technical support; the implementing agency is the government, and NGOs are the implementing partners, not free agents for BE.

When participants discussed the notion of partnership, they provided a general overview of GO–NGO relations in Bangladesh, rather than identifying individual NGO partnerships or ties with GOs. For both organisations, the bond is expectedly spawned from "complementarity," even in a controlled environment where the government remains responsible for providing operational and legal frameworks for NGOs. This complementarity consequently allows for: close interactions; information and resource sharing; increased NGO participation in planning, as well as mutual contributions to development; and adherence to the roles of GOs.[39] Indeed, there are instances of success in development programs in which NGOs are the implementing partners with government agencies. According to Sansom (2011, 290), government initiative and commitment facilitated NGO success in effecting a sanitation program in Bangladesh. In this case, a formal partnership between these organisations facilitated public engagement in a "non-confrontational" and "evidence-based"[40] manner.

That said, research participants verified the existence of collaboration between GOs and NGOs in Bangladesh, and that development policies have created scope for the administrative cooperation required for BE to occur. These findings are also supported by data from secondary sources. Notably, the sixth FYP expands the opportunities for GO–NGO collaboration, especially where the private sector is not specifically interested in not-for-profit development projects (GOB 2012). Partnership with NGOs is also well recognised in the seventh FYP (GOB 2015, 156), which highlights their outreach efforts to deliver education, health and training; encourage female empowerment; and provide both microcredits and social protection, thus establishing these organisations as effective development partners with the government. NGOs have also been considered as one of the driving forces behind the nation's GDP growth by improving human development and reducing poverty. In all, these findings demonstrate a change in perspective, with GO–NGO relations previously deemed as confrontational or "antagonistic."[41]

---

[39] Illustrated in Coston (1998, 362).
[40] The evidence for this is the progress on sanitation and achievement of targets.
[41] Sanyal (1991) described the antagonistic attitude of government officials towards NGO staff or vice versa.

Past FYPs recognised NGOs' ability to reach beneficiaries and create combined opportunities for themselves and GOs to engage communities in national development. GOs often depend on NGOs to engage service recipients, resulting in administrative partnerships during project implementation. Community outreach is an important factor to consider when delivering public services like primary education, primary healthcare services or community capacity building. Here, establishing a connection with local people is instrumental to forging engagement in the development process. Likewise, facilitating strong GO–NGO partnerships streamlines the achievement of prospective development targets. According to one respondent from the government, projects like primary education and health require BE so NGOs work with the government as implementing partners, perhaps carrying out the engagement on behalf of the government. GO–NGO coordination has a positive impact; for example, it enhances better results in health projects, especially in family planning. It is the NGOs' better ability to engage beneficiaries that allows these projects to have higher success rates, even though the NGOs are now less involved than the FWVs, who are working at the grassroots level.

Further considering the advantages of public outreach in remote areas or reaching out to ethnic minorities (for example Dalit communities in the northern part of Bangladesh or tribal communities in the CHT) emphasises above all the benefits of NGO involvement in government projects. An interview with a former CHT project staff member revealed that NGO project implementation is also a way out for government organisations, and a common method for shifting responsibility onto nongovernment bodies to reach the community directly. That said, working with diverse communities in remote areas typically enhances GO–NGO relations, as recognised in development planning. For example, the sixth FYP creates scope for NGOs to work with Dalit communities. The government recognises the need for adequate institutional mechanisms with which to establish links and coordination with both NGOs and private sectors to address issues of ethnic-community development. The same strategy is outlined for the development of people with disabilities. Essentially, NGOs are known to act as the primary entity through which communities are mobilised and target beneficiaries are identified (GOB 2012, 164). The institutional control exercised over NGOs is regarded by GOs (mentioned in the seventh FYP) as one of the main drivers of "creating capacity for the poor and marginalized" (GOB 2016, 46), and not detrimental to the GO–NGO partnership. Tasked with making and measuring practical changes in underprivileged communities, NGOs are used as essentially information vehicles to relay data and feedback to the government, detailing a multitude of results collected across different sectors.

Mutual Dependence in BE

Partnership between GOs and NGOs develops because of mutual dependence, as interviewees observed. Given the advantages and limitations that both GOs and NGOs experience in engaging beneficiaries, these organisations rely on each other to carry out development activities, and this interdependence creates more opportunities for prospective engagement. NGOs are considered as valued partners for GOs. The Perspective Plan of Bangladesh 2021–2041 (GED 2020) recognises NGOs' role in supplementing and promoting development at the grassroots level, for which delivering services to communities is considered critical. As stated in the sixth FYP, the government perceives GO–NGO collaboration as enhancing efficiency in delivering public services, going beyond traditional service sectors in supplying water to slum areas and municipalities, waste management, the rural energy supply, and the creation and development of service and recreational facilities (GOB 2012, 232).

Generally, the purpose of these partnerships ranges from direct focus on service delivery to social empowerment and human development in many developing countries (Haque 2004; Batley and Rose 2011; Alam 2011; Sansom 2011). Here, Bangladesh is not an exception. Batley and Rose discuss how governments and NGOs collaborate on the provision of different services. They argue that NGOs are considered primary alternatives to state-service facilities, where public service is otherwise considered weak (2011, 232). To this, McLoughlin (2011, 241) adds that many NGOs work in collaboration with government bodies to either improve or complement public services. This was repeatedly mentioned in interviews, mainly those with government officials, wherein NGOs are consistently deemed as essential implementing partners in delivering services. Several respondents also emphasised the importance of developing approaches that encourage GO–NGO collaboration geared towards service delivery and improving the capacity development of project beneficiaries. However, the focus is more on expanding service provisions to cover the wide range of citizens in Bangladesh. Given that service delivery is one of the approaches to engaging beneficiaries for their participation, the GO–NGO partnership is also driven by this approach.

As explained by a senior official from the NGOAB, agreement and formal arrangements between GOs and NGOs ensure interconnectivity and coordination, and generally exist in projects for which implementation is entrusted to NGOs. In addition, this interaction is structured from needs realisation to public-service provisions, followed by NGOs providing services to people through public outreach (see Fig. 5.1). Evidently, internal coordination and integration exist between GOs and NGOs and create a scope of interaction with beneficiaries. The relationship between GOs, NGOs and beneficiaries is expected to be interactive, complementary and supportive of each other's role. In turn, this partnership creates coordination between all three groups and encourages ongoing maintenance of the partnership. From this point of view, mutual dependence creates a tripartite link to successful engagement for development participation.

Fig. 5.1. GO–NGO partnership for BE in service delivery

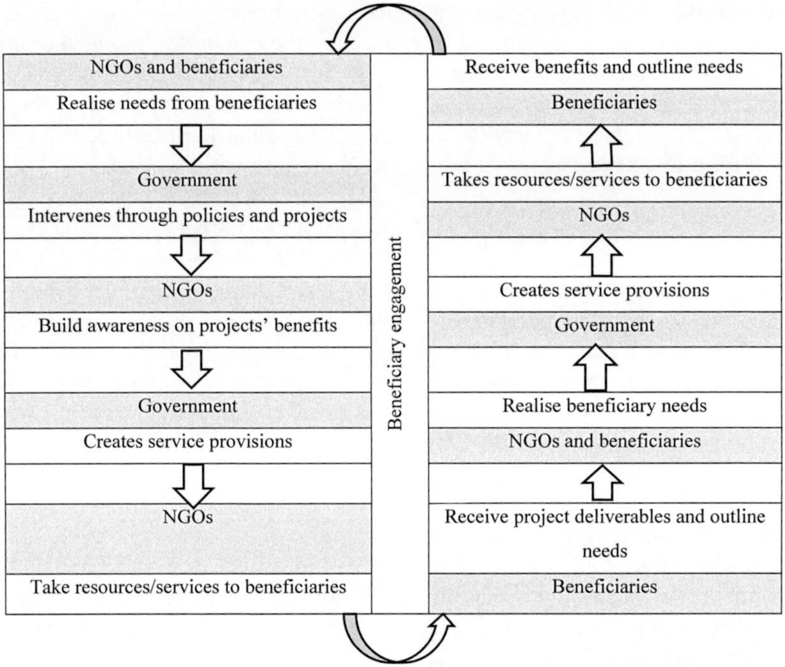

Source: Dutta (2021a)

An NGO executive expressed a similar view, deeming mutual dependence as a tripartite link for successful engagement. He also mentioned that the government's Comprehensive Disaster Management Programme undertaken by the Disaster Management Bureau (DMB) includes community preparedness program volunteers. Here, engaging beneficiaries in the field of disaster management involves NGOs obtaining funds from donors to procure equipment such as umbrellas and megaphones and deliver these to community volunteers. Importantly, the DMB also forms the Union Disaster Management Committee, which develops contingency planning, and whose capacity is developed through NGOs involved in the program.

Partnership with GOs is a Requirement for NGOs

While GO–NGO relations are subject to the latter's reaching the public, NGOs must also actively build a partnership with the government to ensure that BE occurs for participation. Coordination with GOs is necessary when projects are implemented at the field level and where it is a matter of rules, regulations and policy formulation. To Fowler, NGOs need to maintain relationships with stakeholders not only at beneficiary and donor levels, but also with the government, mainly because they operate "along national lines." Thus, maintaining "open space" to function largely depends on what type of "sensitivity" a government has over NGOs in each country context (1997, 116, 121). The need to establish a relational partnership, logically and for a few key reasons, is explicated in the following sections.

Partnership: a prerequisite for NGOs

NGOs are selected through a competitive process that determines whether they can become implementing partners in either government or donor-funded projects. Overall, NGOs with previous work experience with GOs have a competitive advantage when it is a matter of a selection process. The process considers whether the NGO has prior experience of working with GOs and can coordinate with government agencies, as the selection follows the prequalification criteria of a procurement process. Donors also prefer that NGOs have good relations with the government. Similarly, NGOs prefer to maintain relationships with GOs rather than engaging beneficiaries in isolation as this proves their worth to prospective financiers in the competitive-selection process. However, how far this relational partnership is BE-driven or can enhance development participation remains unclear.

NGO independence without GOs on board is undesirable

One of the sections in chapter four illustrated how GOs' authority impacts NGOs in engaging beneficiaries. While it presented interview findings detailing how government authority and endorsement influence BE, there are some examples of successful NGO programs independent of government affiliation. For example, one research participant cited the success of the

BRAC education project and the Grameen Bank projects. Having said that, it seems lone endeavours are not entirely viable for NGOs, as they tend to create tension if the government is not involved. This may threaten the political system or cast BE as a tool for political gain instead of development participation.

Respondents also identified NGO malpractice where government involvement was either limited or absent. However, while advising against potential misdeeds, research participants still maintained emphasis on GO–NGO coordination. According to a project staff member, there had been a risk from independent NGOs like Proshika or Gono Shayajyo Shangstha (GSS), which are known for abusing beneficiaries and compelling them to engage in political campaigns, and misusing assets and funds. It is perceived that NGOs should supplement and be complementary to the government but should not be an independent entity like these NGOs. For GO–NGO collaboration, it is important to see what value is added for engaging NGOs. If BE is to be sustained, the government's involvement is needed and the GO–NGO collaboration can be enhanced, as one research participant suggested.

Upon examining four NGOs in Bangladesh, Ahmad (2002, 120) graded each based on the field worker–client relationship, putting Proshika at the top for its work in motivating and organising landless peoples. Here, Karim (2008, 92) terms the group's activities as part of a "non-party political process," leading to grassroots mobilisation and eventually "putting up candidates for local elections," which worsened GSS–GO relations (Hashemi 1996, 127). The then Grameen Bank chairman wanted to form a political party in 2007 while Bangladesh was ruled by a military-backed caretaker government. Consequently, these NGOs were brought under government scrutiny, which saw both Proshika and GSS deemed dysfunctional entities and the Grameen Bank leadership called into question (Schwittay 2016; Ahmad 2002; Hashemi 1996). Irrespective of research participants' views, GO–NGO partnerships are thus still regarded as desirable opportunities through which NGOs can continue working with project beneficiaries in the development field. Instead of placing them under government scrutiny and creating political tension, the NGO participants interviewed typically preferred to continue their partnerships with GOs in the national-development sectors to which GOs are inextricably bound.

Information on development activities

Regarding service-sector development for subdivisions such as health, agriculture or education, NGOs need to coordinate with government departments at the field level to avoid the duplication of works. Given the role that field administration and UPs play in implementing central-development programs at the grassroots level, NGOs also need to coordinate with these organisations to gather information on projects and align their programs with government initiatives. More specifically, in the agricultural sector, it is important that NGOs work with the DAE so that subsequent engagement initiatives do not overlap. According to one UPZ agriculture officer, NGOs keep in touch with the department for information on development programs in this sector to avoid the duplication of services. This is extremely important for NGOs getting first-hand information from the government to avoid the duplication and redundancy of the project benefits provided. NGOs adjust their project plans based on information obtained from government departments at the field level.

Channelling development funds through GOs

Interviews also revealed that GOs own resources that NGOs need for project implementation if inclusive of BE. As shown in Fig. 5.1, GOs and NGOs partner on service-delivery initiatives. However, to successfully engage people in this regard, NGOs strongly believe that the government's collaboration is both necessary and inevitable, as it is responsible for disbursing the project funds. According to participants, this is because donors prefer funding the government rather than NGOs, as per their mandate to ensure greater cooperation with national governments. In addition, the UN organisations and other donors provide more project funds to the government than ever, which was not the case in the 1980s and 1990s when most, if not all, donor funding flowed directly to NGOs. Donors played a far more significant role in providing financial support and directly backing these activities in exchange for grassroots contacts in Bangladesh (Hashemi 1996, 123). This changed following the Paris Declaration in 2005, which saw increased donor coordination with the government for national development. Moreover, donors are increasingly providing budgetary support (Unwin 2004; OECD 2015) that directly funds government-run development programs in the public sector. It therefore appears that development relations between donors and the government are an unavoidable reality that NGOs cannot ignore.

Despite dwindling direct financial support from donors, BE needs superior project infrastructure to continue developing recipients' skills, for example initiatives around vocational education or technical skills development programs. Here, the research participants believed that GOs represent an essential entity that NGOs must engage with to run these programs. According to one project-management staff, if NGOs do not get the funds for education projects, they cannot run their organisations where GOs are not directly involved. A resource-intensive project like a vocational-education program or the Underprivileged Children Education Program (UCEP) requires GOs to sustain it. UCEP Bangladesh partners with the DWA to develop skills training for women across Bangladesh. It is also linked to the Skills and Training Enhancement Program under the GOB's Technical Education Board. Effectively, this partnership not only provides financial support but is also critical of "further expansion of partnership through networking, brand promotions and having credible references" (UCEP Bangladesh 2016, 17), all of which NGOs need as fuel for their routine functions.

Emerging private sectors

Private-sector investment is contributing to the country's economy, which experienced a sharp increase up to the fiscal year of 2019, though has more recently been highly affected by Covid-19 (Byron and Barua 2021). The loan disbursement is higher than grants received for foreign assistance (see Table 1.1). Private-sector investments are also encouraged for attaining SDGs in Bangladesh (UN 2021). Research participants from NGOs expressed concerns over whether emerging private sectors in Bangladesh are making NGO activities more competitive or less necessary. Similarly, concern looms over UP responsibilities for program implementation at the grassroots level, which might be limiting NGO involvement in engaging beneficiaries within rural communities. Considering these emerging issues in development, NGOs in Bangladesh seem to be strategically expanding partnerships with not only GOs but also private-sector agents, particularly as beneficiaries require different products and services from a range of organisations. In interviews, NGO fieldworkers mentioned that they need to liaise with not only GOs but also private companies, through which they connect people to various services.

Notably, when beneficiaries undertake activities to generate income (such as farming, poultry or livestock), they buy materials such as feed, pesticide and technology to maintain their businesses. For this, NGO partnerships with private sectors yield more benefits for beneficiaries, and NGOs use this approach to ensure beneficiary participation in relevant projects. For example, NGO fieldworkers who were interviewed mentioned that they link beneficiaries with private companies like ACI, Renata and ACME (private industries in Bangladesh) for poultry feed and medicine so that beneficiaries get materials at a cheaper rate than market price.

Partnership with private companies ensures a cheaper rate of these materials for the vulnerable and marginalised beneficiaries. Through the NGO–private sector partnership, the required technology for income-generation activities is also provided to the community. As one NGO executive noted, the emergence of the private sector instigates a sense of competition among NGOs. This inevitably heralds the belief that NGOs need to expand their relationship with the private sector in the process of engaging beneficiaries. Coordination should be between not only the government and NGOs but also GOs, NGOs, and the private sector. During the last two decades, the private sector in Bangladesh has become a competitive force. Like the RMG sector, government subsidies are provided to ensure the optimum benefits. Development planning, which significantly recognises the role of the private sector in national development, has been increasing compared to that of NGOs, as identified in recent FYPs.

UPs: the essential partners for NGOs

Research participants also emphasised coordination and partnership between NGOs and UPs, given the government policies that grant increased responsibility for local development unto the latter. Interviews demonstrated that there should be tripartite coordination[42] between each group, supposedly led by UPs representing the local government at the grassroots level (where beneficiaries are to be engaged in development). Importantly, though, UPs receive block grants from the government because they conduct activities funded by an open-budget system geared towards their direct engagement with project beneficiaries through participatory budgeting.[43] Here, it is equally critical that NGOs have access to UPs while engaging rural communities in project management. Referring to an NGO that had been working on Village Courts and Public Access to Justice for the past twenty-five years, one respondent mentioned that, instead of seeing NGOs function independently in the field, the current ministry–NGO–UP coordination efforts have witnessed improved engagement practises in the implementation of the Activating Village Courts in Bangladesh project.

In Bangladesh, the LGRD ministry actively guides UPs. This means that when development is owned and implemented by the ministry, it becomes mandatory for UPs to deliver project benefits to local communities. Uphoff (1992, 3) said that the term "local" in Bangladesh does not necessarily

[42] Coordination between NGOs, UPs and beneficiaries.

[43] Where a community decides how to spend public money. These are rolled out in municipalities and UPs in Bangladesh. One study found that the scope of participation is low, though the initiative is appreciated (Hossain et al. 2014).

suggest independence at the local level, but is rather "a national government with its own system of local government operating at lower levels." Though decision making takes place at different stages, the UP retains importance (and authority) because participation in local institutions focuses on groups, communities and the locality in which UPs are situated (Uphoff 2014, 4). Evidently then, NGOs need to work closely with these UPs to properly engage project beneficiaries.

Above all, analysis has revealed that different roles and functions determine the nature of GO–NGO relations when BE is attempted, and that cooperation is inevitable. NGOs are not the only organisation responsible for integrating people into development. Instead, UPs are already based on grassroots activities, and private-sector agents are likewise increasing their engagement efforts. As such, NGOs must compete against a range of organisations in joint pursuit to involve communities in national development. This NGO strategy results in a collaborative and complementary relationship rather than NGOs having any conflicts with GOs.

Addressing Opportunities Together

The above discussion demonstrates how the GO–NGO partnership has gradually progressed over several decades. In an environment swayed foremost by governmental control, wherein both regulatory and institutional frameworks determine NGO operations, it is generally believed that significant opportunities still exist for GOs and NGOs to work together towards BE. These opportunities can be categorised into two groups: changes in the role of GOs that are more development focused, and emerging changes in the field of development for which people should be engaged more effectively, as discussed below.

Development thrust in the public sector

There are positive changes in the public sector as civil-service officials are becoming more familiar with development and NGO functions. GOs' positive attitude towards NGOs is characterised by acceptance and recognition of the latter's contribution towards development, as stated in all development policies and planning in Bangladesh. NGO fieldworkers are experiencing changes in attitudes towards NGO staff, and mentioned that the new generation of public-service officials are more open. An NGO participant noted that there is a development thrust in the public sector. The civil service in Bangladesh is expected to carry out government functions and implement policies at the field level with guidelines from respective ministries. While the ministries are headed by public representatives of the political party in power, having the civil service oriented to development is an opportunity to connect people with the government's development agenda. In Bangladesh, NGOs can be seen to be flourishing in the military regime (see chapter two). Accordingly, having GO–NGO coordination under any democratic government will not be detrimental, but rather beneficial to connecting people more to the government functions, especially when NGOs need to partner with GOs for funding, approval and BE at the field level.

Moving forward, digital governance will continue to prove its worth in informing the public about government functions. Government policies, rules and regulations, forms and applications are now available online. Government portals in Bangladesh are contributing to making information accessible, which was not a reality thirty years ago. UISCs at UPs is another dimension of taking services to people at the grassroots level, and is a significant achievement in the country's development field. This is a global trend in connecting people digitally, and Bangladesh is progressing quite quickly in this area that creates more opportunities for making public service responsive. For example, digital portals provide information on development activities, funds and projects available to people, NGOs and private sectors across Bangladesh. Yet the question of the extent to which public queries are addressed remains open.

A full transcript of the Right to Information Act is accessible on multiple government websites, but it remains unclear whether people know which of their rights are outlined in the Act, and this is where BE should be a concern for GOs. Moreover, the issue of a "digital divide" in Bangladesh needs due consideration. The extent to which beneficiaries are capable of handling digital facilities is a question for connecting them digitally. Beneficiaries interviewed and attending FGDs had mobile phones, and in some cases had access to the internet for social media or connecting with their relatives working overseas; rural people go to UPs to use the online facilities; and beneficiaries receive project information via text message. However, BE for development participation is focused on service delivery, providing them access to information (for example, online applications and public-examination results) or communicating development benefits, rather than having beneficiaries participate in the development process. Research participants believed that the GO–NGO partnership can enhance the beneficiary capacity to response to this digital development trend where NGOs can play an important role.

NGOs are the trusted partners of GOs

There are different perceptions on GOs and NGOs in the development context of Bangladesh. In contrast to the negativity that typically shrouds public perception, it has been revealed that both agents view each other positively when development participation matters. For example, one senior NGOAB official revealed that the organisation is comparatively more inclusive of and encourages partnerships with NGOs, as it wants to better understand NGO contributions towards connecting people to development. At the same time, the NGOAB wants to overcome challenges that nongovernment agents typically experience when implementing development programs with GOs and project beneficiaries at the field level. It was said that GO–NGO coordination and the understanding of NGO functions are increasing within the government environment and organisations. For the first time in the history of the NGOAB, workshops were held in seven divisions to enhance the trust, confidence and understanding of NGO activities. NGOAB officials believe that mutual understanding is a must, and mutual respect of each other's work is also to be enhanced.

The pioneering workshops to which the official referred were conducted in 2013, known as The Role of NGOs in the Socio-economic Development of Bangladesh. The subsequent report concluded that the government primarily builds developmental relationships with NGOs on trust. As stated in the report, NGOs in Bangladesh also have profit-making businesses such as banks, insurance companies, universities, shopping centres, and industry, among others, which raises the question of whether they are becoming business organisations. The report said that this is not a problem if NGOs continue working as a "trusted development partner" to the government (NGOAB 2013, 41). Government officials working in the service sector also agreed that having NGOs as implementing partners increases beneficiary involvement, especially with women. One district agricultural official noted that NGOs are supplementary to government agents and play a critical role in facilitating government responsibilities as working intensity for BE increases if NGOs are involved.

Research participants from NGOs also provided similar information, noting that GOs' attitudes towards NGOs have significantly improved. In turn, this has forged opportunities for nongovernment forces to partner with the government on campaigning for greater public involvement. Comparing the advantages of GOs and NGOs (see chapter three) shows how NGOs benefit from GOs in enhancing people's aastha[44]. Upon investigating the

---

44 "aastha" is a Bengali word meaning trust and confidence.

dynamics of developmental partnership (relative to public involvement), NGO research participants appeared more confident in identifying the positive changes in the government. As mentioned in interviews, GOs had negative impressions about NGOs. In some cases, NGO fieldworkers had problems in accessing UPs. NGOs continue to organise meetings with UPs to help them understand that the government cannot undertake development alone. Now there is a development thrust among government officials and the change is visible. NGOs want to grab this change as an opportunity to work with GOs. Further, NGOs are actively implementing government policies to minimise discord between both entities. Changes in government perceptions about NGOs were highlighted in one interview with an executive, who recognised that past GO–NGO distance has been minimised because NGOs are implementing rather than contradicting government policies. Essentially, this reveals that change is both visible and strongly realised by NGOs in Bangladesh, and is regarded as a phenomenon through which to improve GO–NGO relations for engaging beneficiaries.

Changes in beneficiary understanding

As discussed earlier, BE largely depends on how beneficiaries receive and respond to development information. Understanding development benefits plays an important role for beneficiaries to respond to them, which makes BE achievable for both GOs and NGOs at the field level. In addition, public positivity regarding development facilitates and enhances GO–NGO partnerships. The fieldwork revealed that changes have occurred not only at the institutional level but also in people's attitudes towards development programs. Participants from GOs seem to recognise NGO contributions in raising awareness on social issues, thus increasing beneficiary acceptance of development activities. For example, engaging women beneficiaries was challenging, and there were social barriers in the past, as NGO staff had to sit outside the women beneficiaries' houses and speak to them with a curtain separating the parties. Now NGOs have women fieldworkers who can communicate with women beneficiaries, and social barriers are less common when female beneficiaries interact with male staff at GOs or NGOs. The NGOs also communicate with the men in the family, which makes engaging women beneficiaries easier. Government field staff (for example FWVs) also acknowledged changes in beneficiary attitude, which helped to streamline the engagement efforts. While talking about their fieldwork experiences thirty years ago, FWVs mentioned that people used to laugh at them and did not understand anything about their roles. But now if the visit is not done in a month, people – both men and women – keep asking for FWVs. According to one DWA official, female positivity particularly benefits GOs attempting to implement development programs across Bangladesh. It was quite difficult to get women to participate in the past but now they choose to come to the events; the department does not have to work hard to ensure their participation. There is a process of integration in the policies of all ministries, which is why it is possible to mobilise women beneficiaries. Bangladesh has overcome this hurdle to a large extent, and among various platform of women representations, the country also has women's sports teams that compete internationally.

Further, both the socio-economic and cultural contexts matter in the beneficiary perception of participation (Tosun 2000; Kenny 2016), including the rural context of Bangladesh. Having a positive view of development impacts beneficiary perceptions, which not only rationalises BE but also maximises the extent to which the administration can make positive changes. Without proper GO–NGO coordination, groups with vested interests may affect the public attitude and be detrimental to the beneficiaries' attitude in the development process. Hence, during interviews, NGOs expressed concerns over antisocial activities hindering BE, particularly for women. Here, misguided development communication is a risk factor for engaging beneficiaries. Overall, the data demonstrate that GO–NGO partnerships will be limited in situations where NGO–beneficiary relations are affected by any negative social trends. The GO–NGO partnership can create more opportunities for addressing loopholes in development communication through BE and allow meaningful participation to address social problems collectively.

Changes in the development field

It is true that the development achieved in Bangladesh over the last fifty years has been significant. The country has witnessed a multitude of shifts, ranging from receiving food aid to readymade garment (RMG) exports, and from experiencing droughts or lean periods (locally known as "monga") to mobilising a diverse labour force following mass migration to cover economic security, educating underprivileged women about their rights, and securing the government's commitment to increasing public access to information. Overall, respondents perceived these changes as prime opportunities for cultivating development across a diverse range of social, cultural and economic spheres, and further enhancing GO–NGO collaboration for development participation. In the 1980s, development interventions centred around basic services like food and shelter, and the concern for food insecurity was high. The main objective of the development works was to ensure food security. The country has moved far from those basic needs, and what concerns beneficiaries now is ensuring access to services and matters of rights where NGOs can contribute by coordinating with GOs.

GOs and NGOs need to address these emerging changes to extend partnership for enhancing development participation through BE. Issues needing focus now are the pockets of human poverty caused by governance issues, women's empowerment, ensuring women's contribution to decision making, the development of vulnerable groups, Char[45] dwellers and urban poverty. For more than thirty years, FWVs have connected with beneficiaries for contraceptives. It is now time to consider whether other family-welfare issues or health concerns should be included in the BE agenda by GOs, for which NGOs can partner with GOs and ensure the wider participation of people in emerging health issues. For example, there is a need for training on workers' safety, security and employers' positive attitudes, which needs to be conveyed to workers in the RMG sector. NGOs can build capacity through conveying this message to RMG-sector employees, workers and employers for compliance. For rural entrepreneurship and development, it is quite important to tag ICT business branding and link with bigger institutions. NGOs can contribute to that extent, as mentioned by an NGO executive. For governance, certification on VAT and tax is required for rural entrepreneurs where transparency can be ensured if GOs–NGOs and the private sectors are linked, as identified by an NGO executive during an interview.

The scope of the NGO contribution is getting wider and can enhance BE in the development field. As revealed in an interview with an NGO executive, NGO work has been extended to include safe labour migration, which is an important area for BE. Awareness raising can include safe migration, expat workers' safety, remittance reception by rural communities, the development of microfinance entrepreneurship and allowing people to participate in the government's development programs in these areas. Many rural people have access to smart phones, and there are many incidences of social unrest due to the abuse of such facilities. Even awareness raising for the productive usage of mobile phones or the internet is creating opportunities for NGOs to work with GOs to engage beneficiaries at the micro-level. Together, these emerging issues, identified throughout the course of discussions with research participants, are critical for consideration when addressing engagement efforts and determining the relational dynamics (and opportunities, in turn) between GOs and NGOs.

---

[45] A google search provides the definition as "the riverine sand and silt landmasses, home to many people in Bangladesh."

Partnership strengthens GOs' M&E of development

NGOs can potentially partner with GOs to help strengthen their M&E roles. Each of the FYPs recognised the value that GOs invest in M&E as one essential parameter for implementing development policies (highlighted in Fig. 4.1). The government's monitoring is also required to ensure NGO accountability. Strong monitoring can ensure the success of development programs, and the GO–NGO partnership can fill the gap in GOs' monitoring capacity identified in FYPs. M&E can be jointly conducted by GOs and NGOs specifically for the purpose of achieving the development participation that BE leads. Further, the government's monitoring of BE and information on project beneficiaries can offer significant prospects for elevating GO–NGO partnerships. At the same time, M&E in the government should be strengthened to ensure that NGOs effectively engage the public during development initiatives. Overall, NGO activities in this regard would have not been questioned if GOs' monitoring was ensured in partnership with NGOs.

GOs tend to value the M&E skills that NGOs bring to development, as they likely wish to integrate these assets into their own management systems. Subsequent deficiency in monitoring the effect of development on poor and disadvantaged communities (in particular), as well as failure to gauge improvement of ADP implementation, has been repeatedly mentioned in the past FYPs. The need for an effective M&E system is also required to monitor the implementation of these five-year reports themselves. As such, the seventh FYP dedicates a separate chapter to results-based M&E and outlines (GOB 2016, 129) an initiative to formulate a capacity-development results framework (CDRF) based on stakeholder consultation, which includes NGOs along with other organisations. The plan also recognises the importance of GO–NGO relations to strengthen the CDRF process, and partnership is of special importance in an environment of limited capacity to do M&E at the government level. NGOs involved in sectoral programs can provide very helpful information and feedback on results on the ground that "can substantially improve the quality of concerned sectoral M&Es" (GOB 2016, 131). Hence, NGOs' M&E skills are not only recognised in GOs' development planning but also desired for its practical use. It seems that partnering with NGOs on the M&E of development presents an opportunity for GOs to reflect on the extent to which development outcomes are reaching beneficiaries through BE at the grassroots level, which can enhance beneficiary participation in return.

Factors Affecting Partnership on BE

There are emerging issues that affect partnerships and approaches purposed for BE. Notably, there are cross-sectoral ties between private-sector groups or business organisations coupled with the government's approach to maximising national development that will inevitably affect how (and if) people are engaged.

Different development objectives

NGOs experience emerging private-sector groups creating the scope for partnerships with GOs and the private sector that can be geared specifically to BE. However, interviewees expressed concerns about whether private companies share similar objectives to GOs or NGOs. For development to ensue, it is critical that stakeholders have common interests and objectives. If engagement is defined as a process hinged on total participation, it is critical to understand how the private sector will meet this common objective, given its intention to accumulate profit. Discussion with one staff member working on a donor-funded project in Bangladesh, which partners with private organisations to create beneficiary access to markets, noted that managing partnership is a big challenge. The concept, hypothesis and visions are not shared by partner organisations, and business organisations follow ethics, principles and business targets in an informal way, driven by mainly local needs and attitudes, which is different from participatory approaches and strategies envisioned in development concepts and theories. For example, donors have obligations to address gender and nutrition issues, and the project has a component on awareness raising. But partner organisations[46] may not have an obligation to deliver these, as mentioned by the research participants.

This is precisely how GOs and NGOs differ from the private sector. The way that NGOs function – for example, by emphasising a need to empower rural communities, link beneficiaries to public services through direct engagement, and raise funds for community development – wholly contrasts with how private sectors work (Gortner, Nichols and Ball 2007, 25). McLoughlin (2011, 246) stresses the importance of GO–NGO cooperation and the need to share a vision for addressing national development, even when neither group connects via common values or practises. The "fragmentation of meaning between actors" can otherwise impair the prospect of establishing any professional relationship.

[46] Mainly business or profit organisations, as opposed to non-profit organisations.

The above discussion does not necessarily confirm that research participants undoubtedly believe that NGOs are exclusively not-for-profit organisations in Bangladesh. The government's workshop with NGOs nationwide revealed that NGOs also have businesses, though with the objective of improving the living conditions of the poor and marginalised. For example, a female beneficiary (who attended an FGD) in the northern district of Bangladesh said that she had a cheese-production farm, and her product was sold through a value chain, assisted by the NGO. However, the common ground is that the partnership is effective when the development objectives are similar in different organisations. In the absence of similar development visions and objectives of the relevant organisations, partnership becomes difficult for engaging beneficiaries.

Development trends and the GO–NGO partnership

GOs do not undertake development initiatives solely for the service sectors. The more a country grows in terms of its economy, the more its development initiatives are inclusive of mega-projects, including private-sector interventions and infrastructure. Importantly, NGOs are typically not cast as implementing partners in these projects. While the type of project impacts BE (as discussed in chapter three), how far recent development trends at the global and local levels, such as infrastructure development, hold with the concept of people-oriented development requires further investigation. On the other hand, these approaches to development can directly impact the lives of many people (for example, road communication and electricity), which shrinks the concept of development participation though also holds the opportunity for citizens' acceptance and responses to such development in the national context. This is because these interventions certainly impact the lives of people in a positive way: having convenient transportation that helps with marketing goods or supplying electricity to the remotest part of the country makes a difference in the sense of development. Given this recent trend in the country's development, it is believed that the scope of GO–NGO partnerships can be constricted. This is evident in FYPs that emphasised public-investment projects wherein partnerships were routinely established with both local and international private sectors.

This is also a concern for development partners when any change in the regulatory framework creates prospects that affect GO–NGO relations. In addressing recent developments in the Foreign Donations (Voluntary Activities) Regulation Act 2016, concerns were expressed over the provision of punishments to NGOs, outlined in Sections 14 and 15 on offences and the punishment of offences. This recent provision needs some critical examination regarding whether it creates any barriers to establishing complementary relations between the government, development partners and NGOs. It is too early to comment on the act based on the years of the fieldwork (2015–17), and it is not related to research questions already approved for fieldwork. However, NGOs prefer a "complementary" and non-conflicting relationship, with which GOs have no problem. No detrimental incidences under this specific provision of the act or limiting NGO activities at the grassroots level were noted during the fieldwork. BE within the NGO context is thus aligned to this complementarity and without conflict with either GOs or beneficiaries.

An Integrated Approach to Partnership for Engagement

As discussed above, approaches to GO–NGO partnerships for BE have multiple dimensions, and this is not wholly limited to government and nongovernment interventions, but also expands to and incorporates other organisations covering the private sector. It is evident in research findings that GOs, NGOs, donors, private-sector groups, UPs and beneficiaries each play an important role in establishing partnership and coordination for engaging beneficiaries that should result in development participation. It is not a matter of independently securing resources and gaining funding approval or further establishing the capacity and authority for project implementation and public outreach. Rather, a coordinated approach between each entity and asset involved is critical to fostering viable partnerships between organisations and beneficiaries. Evidently, administrative relations seem to be based on well-defined and well-orchestrated organisational roles that are complementary to and supportive of development participation through BE in the country's development context. As such, this is an integrated approach which posits how the individual functions of a concerned organisation are linked to other institutional roles in engaging beneficiaries in the development process. As revealed in interviews and FGDs, Fig. 5.2 describes the expected partnership that research participants think is essential to ensuring development participation. Each entity – GOs, NGOs, UPs, private sectors and beneficiaries – has a role to play if development participation is to be achieved.

Fig. 5.2. Cross-sector partnership for BE

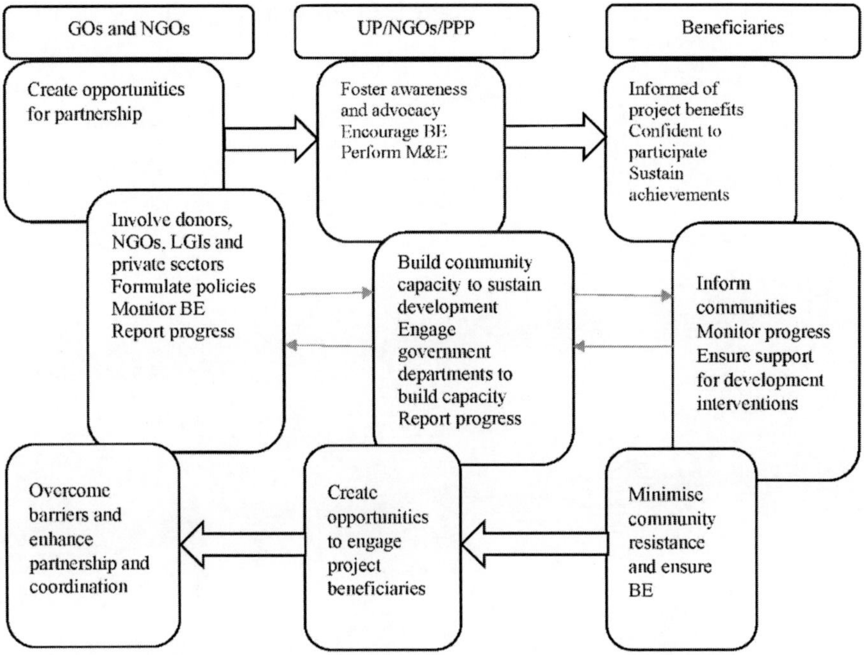

Source: Dutta (2021a)

Overall, given the obvious interdependence and interaction between organisations and project beneficiaries, this chapter has demonstrated that an integrated approach needs to be considered across institutions to transform policy into practice for due engagement in the country's prospective development. However, it is also critical to identify the scope of individual contribution that can be integrated to maximise development participation. An integrated approach is also important for linking cross-sector institutions to beneficiaries. Beneficiaries also have roles to play in fostering their participation in the development. While GO–NGO partnerships are essential in this regard, monitoring is an equally important element to ensure accountability in the wider prospects of BE. This chapter has revealed the dynamics of GO–NGO partnerships that exist or can be fostered according to the BE requirements. These findings contribute to the understanding of the GO–NGO partnership beyond the discussion of relationship, power and the government's control over NGOs, as discussed in the development literature. Along with this, multi-level coordination (Fig. 5.2) and monitoring involving GOs, NGOs, LGIs, the private sector and beneficiaries together are also desired, given their roles in connecting people to development.

CHAPTER SIX

CONCLUSION

People are at the centre of development theories and concepts, and their participation remains at the top of any development interventions taken at the local, national or international levels. The concept of people-oriented development has been evolving for several decades (see Table 1.2), creating the scope for development assistance at the local and national levels. Despite critiques on dependence and colonisation, development assistance is still provided to developing nations, and the government in any country remains responsible for carrying out its development agenda in partnership with development agencies and nongovernment sectors (NGOs, private sector) to deliver development achievements to its citizens. The development literature advocates for people's participation in a local context to localise the development interventions, and organisational roles (such as the government and NGOs) are critical to addressing the local conditions through integrating people into development. This is an ideal context for development concepts. Since each country context is different in its socio-economic and cultural situation, how, when and to what extent people participate in a country's development context require attention. This book has tried to unpack this quest, considering the prerequisite – approaches to BE – for development participation.

This book has also identified the basis for BE in the development context of Bangladesh. Engaging beneficiaries is considered a way of getting people's participation in the development process. This is a common ground that both GOs and NGOs in Bangladesh work within different capacities and scopes of development interventions. While participation has been considered as the key element of orienting people in various development concepts, the discussion in this book has revealed that participation can occur at the micro-level when beneficiaries are engaged within the government and NGO-project settings. Both GOs and NGOs intend to engage people at the grassroots level within the scope of development projects. This approach narrows people to development beneficiaries in each individual project context. That said, development participation does not take place without engaging beneficiaries. Several other factors need to be in place to engage those who in turn believe in participation

Factors Contributing to BE

In the development context of Bangladesh, GOs and NGOs identify strategies to link beneficiaries to development. It starts with their understanding of the terminologies (see Figs. 2.1 and 2.2) along with beneficiaries and their participation. While the scope of the government is wider than NGOs for covering people in general, NGOs work with beneficiaries specific to development interventions and project areas. Despite the colonial influence on government functions and several political changes (military regimes and changes to the democratic government), Bangladesh has experienced development on many fronts and draws international attention by achieving several development targets. At the same time, NGO contributions are well recognised at the national and international levels. Aligning with concepts, people remain at the centre of the country's development planning and policies, allowing both GOs and NGOs working with grassroots-level people to engage them in the country's development process. Being the signatory to various international treatises and declarations is instrumental for both GOs and NGOs to integrate people in formulating development objectives and undertaking development interventions.

The strategies for transferring development policies into practises comprise several factors for engaging beneficiaries and making development participatory. Participation is integrated into the country's development planning and policies that individual ministries and departments remain responsible for implementing. This provision of participation in FYPs creates a scope that both GOs and NGOs find convenient for engaging development beneficiaries while implementing development programs, though it is believed to be an outcome of donor conditions as people-oriented development has been an international agenda set for achievements in different development goals.

Projects are the incubators of development participation, entailing a process of BE that GOs and NGOs undertake. BE provisions in project documents make it easier for both GOs and NGOs to carry it out. Having the provision included in project documents gives it an official concurrence to engage beneficiaries in specific development interventions, such as community development (e.g. projects for the development of Dalit and CHT communities), primary education, health and sanitation. There are service sectors where development interventions cannot be undertaken or continued without beneficiary participation, such as agriculture-extension programs. Development programs cannot be undertaken without participation in this sector as farmers are the owners of land or cultivate on land owned privately by others. They need to cultivate new crops or adopt new technology, for which engaging them is critical. Research participants also agreed that the government's priorities result in speeding up project implementation, which adds an additional advantage for integrating people in the development process. The agriculture sector receives the highest commitment from the government, which the research participants believe to be a critical factor for success in this area. Similarly, mainstreaming women's development across all government ministries and departments has created scope for their participation on various fronts, ranging from cultivation, RMG and the workforce to national and international sports, as mentioned by research participants.

The local administration, including UPs, connects local people to development in the public sector, and NGO presence at the field factors in reaching out to beneficiaries. The local administrative network in the service sectors (for example, health, education and agriculture offices among many others at the district, UPZ and union levels) and service delivery provisions in the UPs are critical for GOs to integrate people in development. Coordination between various government departments and NGOs is essential for connecting beneficiaries. The presence of staff in GOs and NGOs is essential to reaching out to beneficiaries and delivering services so that people are aware of development interventions and can convey their needs, enhance their capacity and participate in providing feedback for monitoring and evaluation. At the grassroots level, community engagement in local-development programs under the Union Parishad Act 2009 and the related rules allows UPs to engage people in their constituencies. Since UPs are providing services in many areas (see chapter two), local communities are more interested in coming to UPs and getting engaged in local development. NGOs equally benefit from the institutional leverages of GOs to engage beneficiaries. Operating within the legal boundaries and control of the government, NGO networks at the grassroots level are crucial for engaging beneficiaries.

However, there is no apparent conflict between GOs and NGOs working with beneficiaries under the government's development agenda stemming from development planning and policies, and guidelines are provided to GOs and NGOs to engage them. Technical expertise, staff presence, having digital facilities at the field level and involving communities and volunteers are considered instrumental in this. There are field staff under relevant ministries who remain responsible for integrating people into development. They are specialised government employees (medical officers or agriculture officers) whose expertise are required to engage beneficiaries participating in the training programs. NGOs seem to utilise these specialised skills to engage beneficiaries. Specialised skills are required for the capacity development of beneficiaries, through which they are engaged. The capacity development of beneficiaries directly contributes to income generation that beneficiaries link to their livelihoods and consider as a reason to participate in these activities. It is important for beneficiaries to connect to service providers, and digital facilities like mobile phones are playing an important role in this. Similarly, UISCs are attracting local communities to connect with UPs as people are more interested in receiving services through using the ICT available there.

At the same time, financial resources are crucial for BE. Given that BE takes place within project contexts, development assistance or government funding is important for implementing project components, which is equally applicable for GOs and NGOs. Funding is not only required for capacity development or income generation, but it also helps in compensating the time beneficiaries spend on engagement activities. In addition, it helps in paying honorarium to experts and committee members participating in BE events. Funding is critical to carrying out microcredit programs, which is one of the significant factors contributing to BE. Thus, project units (within GO and NGO settings) need to have the financial capacity to engage beneficiaries, and the requirements of development assistance are not diminished by the debate on the dependence of underdeveloped nations on developed nations in this regard.

Above all, it is the understanding and responses of beneficiaries of development information that matter for their participation. BE is an essential approach to their understanding and responding to development that can ensure their participation. Communication and interactions within GO–NGO project settings are vital for integrating them in the development process. More specifically, communicating development benefits plays a significant role. Communication has been recognised by GOs and NGOs as a tool for reaching beneficiaries and engaging them. Individual interactions, one-to-one consultations and facilitations at the field level are needed to connect beneficiaries with development projects implemented at the local level. Communicating the benefits allows beneficiaries to receive and respond to development information that impacts their lives and livelihoods. From this point of view, it also impacts BE, whether beneficiaries are receiving positive information about development, if it enhances their socio-economic conditions, and if they want to respond and consequently determine their participation.

The above discussions summarise several factors that are practised to engage beneficiaries in the development context of Bangladesh. Both GOs and NGOs consider BE as a tool to ensure beneficiary participation in the country's development context. As discussed in chapter five, NGOs prefer coordinating and avoiding conflicts with GOs to engage beneficiaries and earn their confidence. At the same time, GOs prefer to partner with NGOs because of their beneficiary outreach and skills essential to engaging rural communities and women. Both these organisations experience advantages and limitations in engaging beneficiaries, and NGOs are not the only entity doing so in the local context. Rather, NGOs need GOs and now reach out to private organisations to connect beneficiaries to their development projects. The government's legal framework or controls do not much affect NGOs if they can work as trusted partners to GOs in the development field. The relationship between GOs and NGOs is one of mutual understanding, coordination and cooperation. NGOs are implementing government policies on development participation and filling out the gaps where GOs do not have adequate resources to achieve it. While the theories and concepts of development argue for integrating people with development through their participation, the practical aspect of participation largely depends on BE, which is subject to several factors, as mentioned above.

BE for Development Participation

The concept of engaging beneficiaries is seldom discussed in development planning; however, the provision of participation in development planning creates demand for engaging them in the Bangladesh context. If the above factors are considered for engagement, it implies that participation follows a process within development projects requiring organisations (GOs, NGOs, UPs, private sectors), staff, technical expertise, communicating development benefits and resources among other things to engage beneficiaries. BE falls within a process entailing projects and is considerably impacted by organisational advantages and limitations. Participation in development can be termed as an "end of spectrum" in which the "voices of citizens are heard and integrated into the state's machineries,"[47] and reaching the end of the spectrum requires "pre-conditions for voices to be heard which require awareness raising and capacity building" (Gaventa 2004, 30) of individual beneficiaries.

[47] As mentioned in this book, government machineries imply various ministries and departments, development planning and policies.

While BE is the prerequisite of development participation, the factors discussed in previous chapters explain how and when beneficiaries are engaged, and the extent to which they participate in the development process is unpacked. BE deals with the process within development projects to ensure participation, and if the process is not addressed, development can lead to a vacuum in participation. As shown in Fig. 6.1, development is meant for the people – citizens at the national level and communities or beneficiaries at the local level – who are expected to participate in development interventions. Development participation needs a process which is inclusive of BE within GO–NGO project settings resulting in participation. The process also requires appropriate strategies that clarify the purpose of engaging the target beneficiaries. This is how BE is shaping up development participation in practice, as identified in this book.

The existing practises of BE in the development field of Bangladesh, as discussed in this book, address the gap between development objectives and participation through the process. Thus, any condition where the process is not present or inadequate will affect development participation. While development participation is presumed to be an outcome of how much beneficiaries are engaged through service delivery, problem identification and needs assessments, or providing microcredits and training, it makes development participation conditional. Any project environment aimed at engaging beneficiaries needs to consider context-specific conditions as well as beneficiary choices to identify strategies to ensure their participation.

At the macro level, the theoretical underpinning of development involves citizens, communities and beneficiaries in illustrating the need for people-centred development and people's participation. The inclusion of people is wide and involves large numbers in its concept. This wider perspective is narrowed to the local context where target beneficiaries are expected to be involved in projects through a process that should result in their participation. In the Bangladesh context, the government, NGOs and private sector are contributing to fill out the process part; however, not all processes include BE for development participation. It depends on what type of project is undertaken, whether it draws from the development budget or revenue budget, and whether formats and templates allow BE. While development participation is narrowed to projects, this much-discussed concept is at risk of not achieving participation in the absence of projects and associated factors, as discussed in this book.

Fig. 6.1. Development process and BE for participation

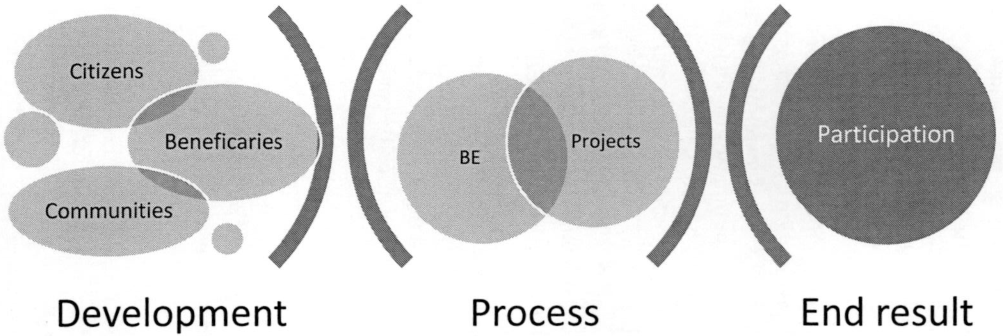

Source: Dutta (2021a)

In the process of achieving participation, BE is understood as a way of participation in problem identification, needs assessment and the collection of data on health issues in the planning phase of development interventions. Beneficiaries obtain opportunities to convey their needs and concerns based on the development intervention designed by government ministries or NGOs individually to seek project funds. Participation at this stage is defined as people communicating their needs and problems to organisations responsible for undertaking development interventions. Field staff visit households, talk to families and organise meetings with communities to gather beneficiary views on problems to be addressed by GOs or NGOs through development projects. Their voices are heard in these ways. Development participation is perceived as a way of mobilising beneficiaries for project launch events, workshops, consultations, courtyard meetings and capacity-development training. These approaches are important because they create opportunities for beneficiaries to obtain information relevant to their lives and livelihoods, and to determine their participation. For example, they participate in income-generation activities, and tend to receive tangible benefits from development programs like agriculture, tailoring, livestock or poultry farming and small entrepreneurship. From beneficiary and GO–NGO points of views, this is how they are engaged and participate in the development process. The country has seen successes in many areas such as women's development, sanitation, agriculture production, reducing child mortality, microcredits, primary education and disaster management that collectively and gradually contribute to upscaling the country's socio-economic conditions since independence. Approaches to BE that GOs and NGOs practise directly contribute to participation and achievements in these areas.

Findings from interviews and FGDs demonstrate that BE is effective if it is considered a priority by the government. Thus, development participation has to be a priority of the government at the national level to help GOs and NGOs engage beneficiaries, otherwise the scope of participation may be minimised. BE is a guided activity for GOs and NGOs. Guiding principles are desired because the country has seen NGO activities as threats to the government through being independent in mobilising beneficiaries for political interests. Therefore, NGOs think coordination and cooperation between GOs and NGOs are critical for engaging beneficiaries for their participation. NGOs align with the government's development agenda and avoid conflicts in running programs without any complications, for example working in the field without resistance or getting funds or approval of foreign aid. GOs prefer trusted partners to carry out development programs. It is important to note that the development agenda at the grassroots level does not differ much between GOs and NGOs. For example, GOs invest in women's development, education, health, and capacity development where NGOs work. On the other hand, NGOs track government policies to discover the development agenda where NGOs can fill in.

However, within this mutual dependence to eliminate challenges, understanding how far beneficiaries participate in the development process remains critical. Participation requires organisations, strategies, community-engagement activities, locational context and management to build relations between development interventions and beneficiaries. It also requires establishing links between institutions, for example partnership between GOs, NGOs, UPs, private sectors, donors and beneficiaries. But any of these can be delinked if the conditioning factors are not addressed and objectives are not aligned to participation. Furthermore, there is the possibility of losing the priority of participation, NGOs not being a trusted partner to GOs, changes in the development agenda, and having donors with no objective of development participation or bias in UPs, given that their political affiliation cannot be denied. BE requires resources. What if resources are not available in the form of projects usually including BE for development participation? All these will have impacts on BE in practice, and consequently can limit the scope of development participation. A leading newspaper recently reported on how the village courts functions are being disrupted by the absence of a project and waiting for funding from the government (The Daily *Prothom Alo* 2022). Bangladesh aims at becoming an upper-middle and high-income country by 2031 and 2041, respectively. Thus, development is led more by private-sector investments than by grants, which were significantly low in FY 2020–1 (see Table 1.1). This low level of grants can impact development participation as BE requires resources. Aligning to the development objective is essential for engaging beneficiaries if their participation is to be ensured.

The Extent to which Beneficiaries Participate

Participation creates the ground for raising people's voice and "putting the last first," as discussed in development theories. The concept of participation is also expected to be a "voluntary" contribution to development interventions. In practice, people do participate when they are engaged, they find it relevant to their lives and livelihoods, and their participation is ensured within a GO–NGO project setting. Bangladesh is an example of how development planning and policies in the public sector allow NGOs to work with people and create opportunities for beneficiaries to participate in development interventions. For GOs and NGOs, participation has to count on beneficiaries receiving services, training and communications and participating in project activities. Thus, the government and NGOs, together or individually, accomplish the most difficult part of the development process, which is engaging beneficiaries. The planning in Bangladesh values integrating people into development and continuing the inclusion of marginalised and vulnerable communities in the interventions. The gradual social inclusion of the Dalit community (see Box 3) or development of tribal communities in the CHT are two examples of many. It is a reality in Bangladesh that rural women are involved in entrepreneurship and small businesses. They own land, tailoring shops, cheese factories, poultry and livestock through either microcredit programs or obtaining services from GOs and NGOs. Their participation in these project activities leads to these development achievements of improving socio-economic conditions.

However, BE for development participation largely depends on how beneficiaries receive and respond to development. People tend to see the tangible outcome of development, for example training to upscale skills, high yielding crops for farmers, or income generation through small business and entrepreneurship through which they participate in the development process. It is the beneficiaries' choice, capacity and acceptance of development that ultimately shape up their participation. Development benefits need to be communicated for which organisational set up, monitoring and resources (both human and financial resources) are inevitable. However, understanding only development benefits can be problematic in a condition where monitoring is not strong enough to control exploitation and so affects people's lives. When marginalised people in Bangladesh invest in so-called financial scams or become victims of human trafficking, their understanding of the benefits means that they want to connect to the improvement of their economic conditions. Their participation is misguided, and at the same time their attention to development benefits can be diverted in a context with little or no monitoring. This raises questions over whether beneficiaries (or citizens at the macro level) can be engaged in the absence of tangible benefits or financial assistance, or if no specific project is planned. If not, then development participation will be limited or difficult to achieve in the broader spectrum. Not all development benefits, such as climate change and environmental sustainability, good governance and democratic practises that are pertinent to twenty-first century growth are readily perceivable. Hence, GO–NGO approaches to engaging beneficiaries and beneficiary responses to the development agenda will determine their participation.

While service provisions in the GOs or NGOs is an approach to BE, it is critical to understand whether beneficiaries are involved in receiving services or creating demands on the state to design services meant for them. The decentralisation of service provisions and local administrative networks is important to beneficiaries as they prefer to connect with service providers, for example UPs. In its practical application, development participation is related to receiving services, such as getting internet access, necessary government forms and applications, or receiving rice at a low price provided by the government. Here participation counts on people's access to services or how many beneficiaries are availing these services, which limits their active participation in driving the development agenda. Research participants identified agriculture, health, education, youth development, disaster management and women's development as some of the key public-sector areas where BE has ensured their participation in line with the government's development planning. However, these are not the only areas which the public sector is responsible for delivering services. It includes the whole range of service provisions for people. Whether all the sectors equally value beneficiary (or rights holder) engagement for development participation can be questioned. Answering this is not possible in a PhD study, though this book presents some important contexts where beneficiaries are engaged, resulting in their participation in the development process.

It is important for NGOs to receive project funds from either the government or donors to continue engaging beneficiaries. NGOs prefer to coordinate with the government, which allows these organisations to work in the development field without any difficulties in engaging beneficiaries. The partnership between GOs and NGOs maximises the advantages and minimises the limitations that these entities experience in integrating people into development. Thus, BE is guided considering the mutual dependence between GOs and NGOs, and so is development participation which aligns with project reporting and fulfilling the requirements of formats and templates. BE settings also differ within revenue and development budget projects, though formats and templates for reporting in the government projects include sections for beneficiary feedback. BE is context specific; there is no one approach to BE that will work for all communities or people in different geographical locations of the country.

Development participation can thus vary in different contexts within the same country. However, development participation should not be measured according to the reporting tools. NGOs have websites that showcase the improvements achieved by beneficiaries through their participation. These are undeniable facts, and improvement in beneficiaries' lives is visible. Having said that, this visibility does not provide any picture of participation beyond the project lifecycle. In addition, how these beneficiaries are affected in times of natural disasters, social unrest or change of political control is not clear. How farmers survive when they lose crops due to floods and how this affects their participation is also very hard to discern from the government or NGO websites. What happens to beneficiaries if they cannot repay loans and how this failure affects their participation are other areas that need attention to define development participation.

One of the challenges is corruption, which can limit the scope of BE, as mentioned by research participants. Understanding, interpreting and responding to development benefits through project communication have been instrumental for BE. However, it will be challenging to determine how beneficiaries will set their own priorities. For example, whether the need for primary education or public-health maintenance will be understood over poverty alleviation and if beneficiaries will participate remain unknown (Dutta 2021b). As evident in the research findings, beneficiaries tend to become disengaged if they cannot align development interventions with their priorities. Communicating and understanding only micro-level development benefits may create loopholes, such as corruption, and make it more challenging for beneficiaries to make choices between short-term benefits and long-term development goals. There is a risk of being exploited rather than engaged in the development process as beneficiaries are exposed to not only project communication but also multiple sources of communication, and have opportunities to align these with their priorities. For example, despite the policies in place, people are victims of human trafficking, financial scams or fraudulent activities. Exposure to these malpractices can minimise the scope of people-oriented development or the extent to which beneficiaries can participate in the development process.

At the same time, aligning development benefits to beneficiary's needs makes them reliant on the state instead of having their say in decision making or participating voluntarily in the development process. Their active participation is limited in that sphere. On one hand, this creates an opportunity for the service providers to deliver development benefits in line with beneficiary demands and maintain the beneficiaries' achievements. Keeping citizens at ease with the development benefits this way may give the government an opportunity to receive unquestioned support from people. On the other hand, it risks the stability due to discontentment, and in any case it fails to realise the development benefits mainly when implementation (if not pro-people) of development agenda do not comply pro-people policies. This scenario will limit beneficiary participation. This approach also limits the scope of engaging beneficiaries in addressing diverse development issues that affect their lives, for example workplace safety for garment workers, safe migration, tax coverage, utilising internet facilities to receive and respond to productive information, and raising concerns over malpractice in organisations including NGOs. These are some areas that research participants considered as emerging issues for which BE is essential to achieving participation. Focusing only on beneficiary needs to align development projects for development participation will miss the opportunity to address the reality of these emerging issues.

The discussion has also identified donor influence or preference as a powerful force of influence. Although GOs and NGOs seem to (increasingly) comply with donors' requirements for BE, the question is whether all partners in the country's development share the same preferences. Development is governed by trends and moves fast at the global level, with which the local context needs to match itself. Development concepts including participation in its process are driven by contemporary issues, which has been evident since the 1940s (see Table 1.2). This also changes the trends of development in the local context. The reality of development trends is obvious while development assistance is received for mega-projects, such as the creation of powerplants, bridges and infrastructure, and building roads and highways. Certainly these mega-projects help with improving the standard of living. Beneficiaries can see the impact of such development on their daily lives, for example commuting efficiently or having electricity – an essential commodity to their income-generation activities. People still need to be engaged to participate in this wider perspective of development where they can contribute to safe commuting or energy saving. The current practice of micro-level project-based engagement is also missing the bigger picture of development that the country is going through. Whether donors routinely consider engagement in relation to these forms of development cannot be understood without any activities in place. In addition, BE required for development participation is a resource-intensive approach.

There is a need for financial resources for GOs and NGOs to engage beneficiaries. Absent or inadequate development assistance will result in limited or no development participation in the current practises. While donor agreements lead to BE, as is evident in discussions in this book, the absence of this strategy in the donor agenda will impact development participation. The recent development targets are outlined in SDGs that have added the potential for social mobilisation and securing interaction between diverse stakeholders (Miller-Dawkins 2014), and funding is equally critical to their success. However, resources are not adequate for meeting these targets in developing or least-developed countries (Reality of Aid report 2018, 7). Achieving SDG targets without involving beneficiaries is not a desired condition for fulfilling the requirements of development participation.

To conclude, Bangladesh is a unique example of gradual progression in terms of development achievements. Development planning and policies consider the inclusion of people and delivering the development benefits to the marginalised and vulnerable, which allows GOs and NGOs to work with people and ensure their participation in the development process. However, participation is subject to how beneficiaries are engaged within GO–NGO project settings at the micro-level of development. This is a process that results in participation when enabling factors are present. GOs and NGOs partner together to address the challenges associated with BE to enhance development participation. It is important to revisit the concept of participation given its sole focus in practice on tangible outcomes within project settings. This approach will affect participation in achieving development agendas like climate change or environmental sustainability that have long-term benefits for development. The importance of engaging beneficiaries should not be ignored and needs to be supported to not only make development people-oriented, but also critically make people development-oriented for their participation.

Appendix A
Different Project Types in the Development Context of Bangladesh

Projects are divided into seven categories:

(1) **Investment projects**: these include capital investments such as the construction of roads, bridges and powerplants.
(2) **TA projects**: these are usually funded by donors, with production costs either fully or partially met by foreign aid.
(3) **Service-sector projects**: these offer social benefits, for example education, health and sanitation.
(4) **Self-financing projects**: these generate resources in the industry or production sectors.
(5) **Non-revenue earning projects**: these accrue benefits to other parties, including water and irrigation projects.
(6) **Regional TA projects**: these are intended for certain regions (including Bangladesh) but are not nationally financed.
(7) **Private-sector TA projects**: these are received through the ERD.

Source: GOB (2016, 1–22); GED (2014, 4)

Appendix B
Government and NGO Approaches to Engagement

Approach to engaging	Participants from GO	Participants from NGOs
Scope of engaging	Engaging beneficiaries is subject to specific situation and context.	Government departments work directly with beneficiaries. When government departments work directly with beneficiaries that implies that beneficiaries are engaged.
	Beneficiary engagement is contextual as and when required.	Beneficiary engagement is a token.
	Beneficiaries are engaged by government where there is a direct interaction with people.	Beneficiaries are engaged through the target-group approach – beneficiary groups are formed, and these groups are linked to service-provider agencies, either GOs or NGOs.
Management	BE implies decentralisation.	Working closely with beneficiaries is BE
	BE means to inform beneficiaries about the project and its impacts.	Creating volunteers and providing equipment to manage community issues like disaster management. Here BE is capacity development of the target population. It is a method of knowledge transfer.
	Engaging local people is a method to BE as local people know the local needs.	BE starts with social mapping, baseline survey and needs realisation.
	Engagement means to mobilise participants to project events.	Beneficiaries are engaged through the target-group approach. Beneficiary groups are formed, and these are linked to service-provider agencies, either GOs or NGOs.

Approach to engaging	Participants from GO	Participants from NGOs
	Working together is to make engaging beneficiaries happen.	Identification of beneficiary needs.
Outreach	BE means giving door-to-door visits to beneficiaries.	NGO staff moving around the specific locality to identify beneficiaries – apply case management strategy.
	BE means going to people.	BE means reaching beneficiaries.
	Engaging women requires rigorous involvement and contact to their families.	If it is engaging women beneficiaries, it is equally required to engage their male counterparts in the family.
	Getting in touch with people is engaging.	BE means assessing basic needs by reaching beneficiaries.
		BE means going into the field every day
Interaction	To let people know what benefits the project will bring to them.	BE means sitting with beneficiaries and talking to them to identify their areas of interventions.
	BE means convincing beneficiaries.	It requires personal and one-to-one communication.
	BE means having huge interactions with beneficiaries.	BE means conveying information to beneficiaries.
	BE means communicating with beneficiaries.	BE means day-today interaction with people.
	Engaging is a kind of everyday dealing with beneficiaries.	BE means assessing basic needs by reaching beneficiaries.
	BE means having interaction, networking, professional and personal relationship with beneficiaries.	
	BE means having campaign and communication.	
Empowerment	BE means social inclusion.	Engaging beneficiaries ensures their access to services.
	BE means sharing benefits with target population.	BE means ensuring beneficiary rights.

Approach to engaging	Participants from GO	Participants from NGOs
	BE means building trust between government and beneficiaries, getting their confidence. BE means minimising distance between these two groups.	
	BE means having a culture of accumulation and accommodation of diverse opinions.	
	It is kind of building long-term relationship.	
Capacity development	BE means raising awareness.	BE means capacity development of the target population.
	Internet service is a way to engage beneficiaries.	BE is a method of knowledge transfer.
	Providing technical advice is to engaging beneficiaries.	

APPENDIX C
RELATIONS BETWEEN PROJECT AND BE

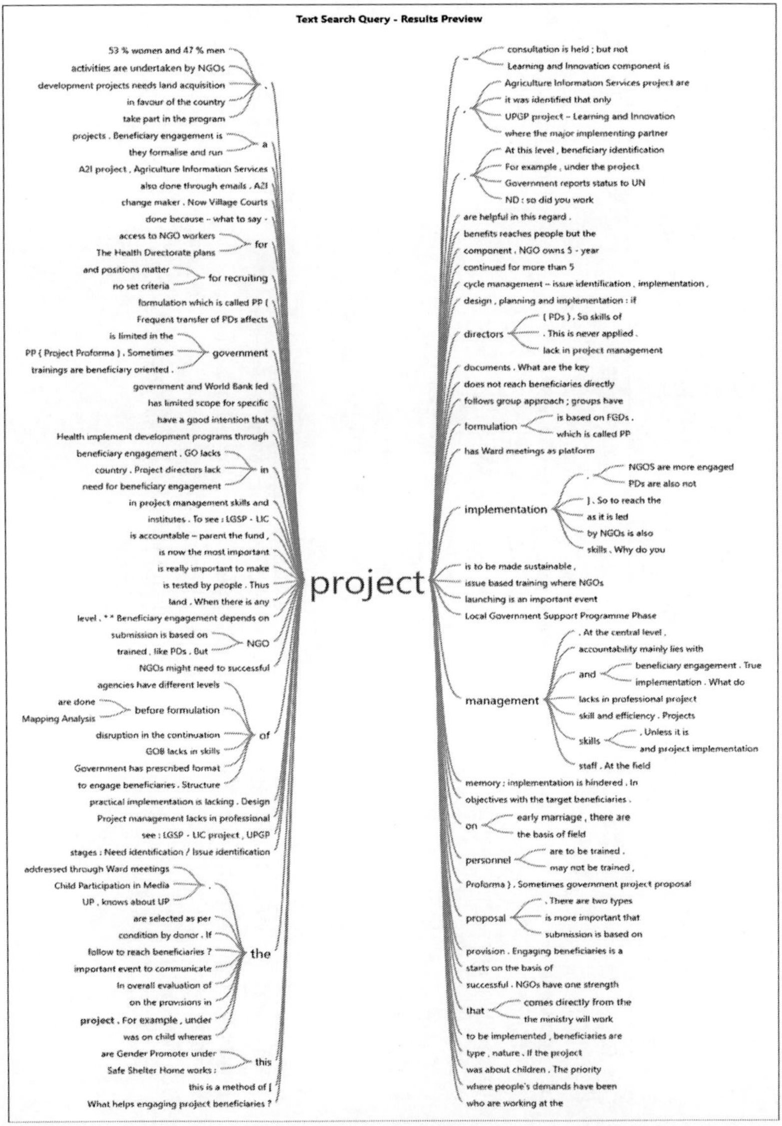

APPENDIX D

PEOPLE AND DEVELOPMENT IN PUBLIC-SECTOR TRAINING

Institutions	Category of trainees	Development focus	People focus
Bangladesh Public Administration Training Centre (BPATC)	Civil servants from new entrants to senior levels	• Project-management basics • Theories and concepts • Development planning • Public-service management and governance, NPM • Development administration • Behavioural aspect of public-service management • SDGs	Service delivery to citizens
National Academy for Planning and Development (NAPD)	Civil servants from economic cadre Other government officials Private-sector employees	• Skills of development planning and implementation in the public sector • Project-management basics • Technical skills, such as project M&E	Design and implement development programs for citizens

The National Institute for Local Government (NILG)	LG representatives LG officials from public services	• Relevant laws, rules and regulations of local-level planning and development • Social issues like anti-terrorism activities • Participatory approach to development	Integrating people in local-development planning and implementation
Bangladesh Academy for Rural Development (BARD)	Civil servants, NGO staff and beneficiaries	• Rural development • Participatory approach to development • Social development • Agriculture development • Employment generation	Capacity building or project beneficiaries; inclusion of communities in development
Rural Development Academy (RDA)	As above	As above	Gender equality and women's development; building a change agent in rural development

Source: adapted from training modules available on BPATC, NAPD, NILG, BARD and RDA websites

APPENDIX E
INSTITUTIONAL INTERACTION THROUGH FORMAL COORDINATION

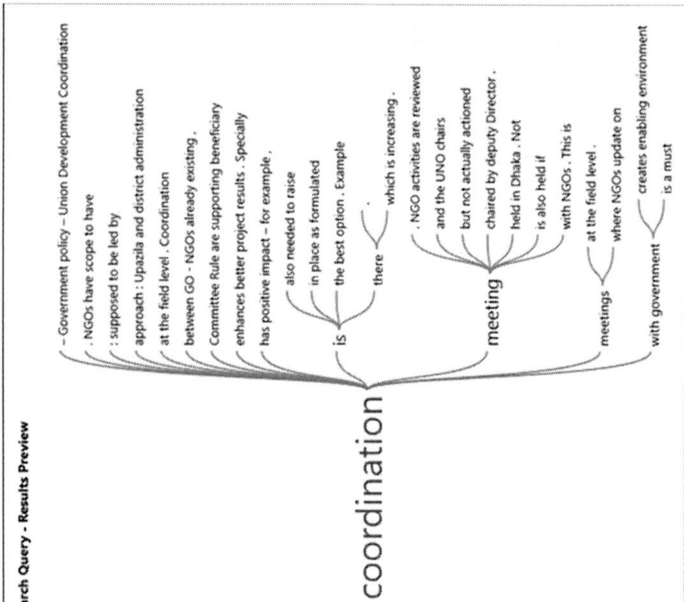

References

Abraham, A. 2014. *Project Planning and Management: An Aspect of Development*. Germany: Verlag.

Ahmad, M. M. 2002. *NGO Field Workers in Bangladesh*. Farnham, Surrey: Ashgate Publishing.

Ahmed, S. and M. Rafi. 1999. 'NGOs and Evaluation: the BRAC experience'. Paper presented at World Bank Conference: Evaluation and Poverty Reduction, Washington, D.C., 14–15 June.

Alam, S. M. N. 2011. 'Health Service Delivery: The State of Government–Non-government Relations in Bangladesh'. *Public Administration and Development* 31: 273–81. doi: 10.1002/pad.608.

Alesina, A. and D. Dollar. 2000. 'Who Gives Foreign Aid to Whom and Why?' *Journal of Economic Growth* 5: 33–63.

Amin, S. B. and M. Murshed. 2017. 'International Fund Inflows, Economic Growth and Health Care Development: The Case of Bangladesh'. *Journal of Accounting, Finance and Economics* 7(1): 103–117. https://papers.ssrn.com/sol3/papers.cfm?abstract_id=3070163

Apeldoorn, B. van, and H. Overbeek. 2012. 'Introduction: The Life Course of the Neoliberal Project and the Global Crisis'. In *Neoliberalism in Crisis*, edited by H. Overbeek and B. van Apeldoorn. Hampshire: Palgrave Macmillan.

Arvelo, W. 2012. 'College Consortia: Engaging In and Sustaining Community Collaboration Efforts'. Doctoral thesis, University of Massachusetts Boston, ProQuest dissertations and thesis database.

ASA n. d. viewed 14 April 2018, www.asa.org.bd.

Askew, I. and A. R. Khan. 1990. 'Community Participation in National Family Planning Programs: Some Organizational Issues'. *Studies in Family Planning* 21(3): 127–42. http://www.jstor.org/stable/1966712.

Awortwi, N. 2013. 'The Riddle of Community Development: Factors Influencing Participation and Management in Twenty-Nine African and Latin American Communities'. *Community Development Journal* 48(1): 89–104. doi: 10.1093/cdj/bsr071.

BBS (Bangladesh Bureau of Statistics) 2022. *Statistical Pocket Book 2021*. Dhaka: Government of People's Republic of Bangladesh.

Bangladesh Financial Intelligence Unit. 2015. 'NGO/NPO Sector Assessment of Bangladesh'. https://www.bb.org.bd/pub/research/sp_research_work/srw1505.pdf.

Banglapedia. 2015. 'Budget, Government', viewed 23 November 2019. https://en.banglapedia.org/index.php?title=Budget,_Government.

Banglapedia. Online. 'Dalit Community', viewed 23 December 2022. https://en.banglapedia.org/index.php/Dalit_Community

Bardhan, P. 2002, 'Decentralization of Governance and Development', *Journal of Economic Perspectives* 6(4): 185–205.

Bassler et al. 2008. *Developing Effective Citizen Engagement: A How-To Guide for Community Leaders*. Pennsylvania: The Centre for Rural Pennsylvania.

Batley, R. 2011. 'Structures and Strategies in Relationships between Non-government Service Providers and Governments'. *Public Administration and Development* 31(4): 306–19. doi: 10.1002/pad.606.

Batley, R. and P. Rose. 2011. 'Analysing Collaboration between Non-governmental Service Providers and Governments'. *Public Administration and Development* 31(4): 230–39. doi: 10.1002/pad.613.

Berg, B. L. 2004. *Qualitative Research Methods for the Social Sciences* (5th edition). Boston: Pearson.

Boston, J. 2011. 'Basic NPM Ideas and Their Development in Christensen'. In *The Ashgate Research Companion to New Public Management*, edited by T. Christensen and P. Lægried. Surrey: Ashgate Publishing.

Boswell, J., S. Catherine and A. Dugdale. 2014. 'Who Speaks, and in What Voice? The Challenge of Engaging "The Public" in Health Policy Decision Making', *Public Management Review* 17(9): 1358–74. doi: 10.1080/14719037.2014.943269.

BRAC (Bangladesh Rural Advancement Committee) Learning Division. n. d. 'Training Principles', viewed 14 April 2018. http://learning.brac.net/.

BRAC. n. d. 'Who We Are', viewed 14 April 2018. www.brac.net.

BTRC. n. d. 'Mobile Subscribers', viewed 18 August 2019. http://www.btrc.gov.bd/content/mobile-phone-subscribers-bangladesh-june-2018.

Bryman, A. 2008. *Social Research Methods* (3rd edn). New York: Oxford University Press.

Buba, I. A. 2019. 'Aid, Intervention, and Neocolonial "Development" in Africa', *Journal of Intervention and Statebuilding* 13(1): 131–38. doi: 10.1080/17502977.2018.1470136.

Byron, R. K. and D. Barua. 2021. 'Private Investment Hits a Trough'. The *Daily Star*, 8 August 2021. https://www.thedailystar.net/business/economy/industries/investments/news/private-investment-hits-trough-2147471.

Campbell, M. and A. Hoyle. 1990. 'The Vicissitudes of Development Administration'. In *Government and People: Issues in Development*, edited by M. Campbell and A. Hoyle. Canberra: University of Canberra.

Caporaso, J. A. 1980. 'Dependency Theory: Continuities and Discontinuities in Development Studies'. *International Organization* (34)4: 605–28. https://www.jstor.org/stable/2706514.

Chambers, R. 1984. *Rural Development: Putting the Last First*. New York: Longman.

—. 1994. 'The Origins and Practice of Participatory Rural Appraisal', *World Development*, 22(7): 953–69.

—. 1997. *Whose Reality Count? Putting the First Last*. London: Intermediate Technology Publications.

Clark, J. 2006. 'Democratising Development: NGOs and the State. *Development in Practice* 2(3):151–62. doi: 10.1080/09614524920007799l.

Cons, J. and K. Paprocki. 2010. 'Contested Credit Landscapes: Microcredit, Self-Help and Self-Determination in Rural Bangladesh'. *Third World Quarterly* 31(4): 637–54, doi: 10.1080/01436591003701141.

Conyers, D. 1984. 'Decentralization and Development: A Review of the Literature'. *Public Administration and Development* 4: 187–97.

Cooke, B. and U. Kothari. 2001. 'The Case for Participation as Tyranny' In *Participation: the new tyranny?,* edited by B. Cooke and U. Kothari. London: Zed books.

Coomaraswamy, I. 2012. 'Overview of Global Reforms in Foreign Aid'. In *Foreign Aid in South Asia: The Emerging Scenario*, edited by S. Kelegama. Delhi: SAGE.

Corbridge, S. 2002. 'Development as Freedom: The Spaces of Amartya Sen'. *Progress in Development Studies* 2(3): 183–217. doi: 10.1191/1464993402ps037ra.

Coston, J. M. 1998. 'A Model and Typology of Government-NGO Relationships'. *Nonprofit and Voluntary Sector Quarterly* 27(3): 358–82. doi: 10.1177/0899764098273006.

Crush, J. 1995. *Power of Development*. London: Routledge.

Devas, N. and U. Grant. 2003. 'Local Government Decision-Making—Citizen Participation and Local Accountability: Some Evidence from Kenya and Uganda', *Public Administration Development* 23(4): 307–16. doi: 10.1002/pad.281.

Dutta, N. 2021a. 'Engaging project beneficiaries: a comparative analysis of government and NGO practices in the development context of Bangladesh'. PhD Thesis. University of Canberra.

Dutta, N. 2021b. 'Communicating Development Benefits: an approach to beneficiary engagement and post-pandemic challenges'. *2021 NAASPA South Asia Conference*. 12-14 November 2021. Dhaka: North South University

ERD (Economic Relations Division). n. d. 'Flow of External Resources into Bangladesh 2011-2012', viewed 22 July 2013. www.erd.gov.bd/site.

—. n. d. 'Flow of External Resources into Bangladesh 2015-2016', viewed 6 March 2019. https://erd.gov.bd/site/page/84648784-9e8a-4760-8e47-6d20ad3013a8/flow-of-external-resources-into-bangladesh-2015-2016.

—. n. d. 'Overall Scenario of Foreign Assistance Management FY 2021-22', viewed 21 December 2022. http://www.erd.gov.bd/site/page/9a23bb25-5ff7-421b-8a73-b7c6b33c8032

Escobar, A. 2010. 'Worlds and Knowledges Otherwise: The Latin American Modernity/Coloniality Research Program'. In *Globalization and Decolonial Option*, edited by D. W. Mignolo and A. Escobar. Oxon: Routledge.

Eversole, R. 2010. 'Remaking Participation: Challenges for Community Development Practice'. *Community Development Journal* 47(1): 29–41. doi: 10.1093/cdj/bsq033.

Fowler, A. 1997. *Striking a Balance: A Guide to Enhancing the Effectiveness of Non-governmental Organizations in International Development*. London: Earthscan Publications.

Führer, H. 1996. *The Story of Official Development Assistance: A History of DAC/DCD in Dates, Names and Figures.* Paris: Organisation for Economic Co-operation and Development.

Fukuda-Parr, S. 2004. 'Millennium Development Goals: Why They Matter'. *Global Governance* 10(4): 395–402. https://www.jstor.org/stable/27800537.

Gaventa, J. 2002. 'Introduction: Exploring Citizenship, Participation and Accountability'. *IDS Bulletin* 33(2): 1–11.

—. 2004. 'Towards Participatory Governance: Assessing the Transformative Possibilities'. In *Participation from Tyranny to Transformation? Exploring New Approaches to Participation and Development*, edited by S. Hickey and G. Mohan, London: Zed Books.

Gaventa, J. and C. Valderrama. 1999. 'Participation, Citizenship and Local Governance'. Background note: *Strengthening Participation in Local*

Governance Workshop. Institute of Development Studies, 21–24 June 1999.

GED (General Economics Division). 2014. *Development Project Proforma/Proposal (DPP) Manual Part 1: Main Guideline*. Dhaka: Ministry of Planning.

—. 2020. *The Perspective Plan 2021-2041*. Dhaka: Ministry of Planning.

GOB (the Government of Bangladesh). 1972. *The Constitution of the People's Republic of Bangladesh*. Dhaka: Government of Bangladesh.

—. 1995. *The Fourth Five Year Plan 1990-1995*. Dhaka: Planning Commission.

—. 2012. *The Sixth Five Year Plan FY2011-FY2015*. Dhaka: Planning Commission.

—. 2015. *Guidelines for Annual Performance Agreement (2014-2015)*. Cabinet Division. http://cabinet.portal.gov.bd/sites/default/files/files/cabinet.portal.gov.bd/page/089de62d_b4d1_4aa7_a879_bc9d483d9b2c/APA%20GUIDELINES%202014-15%20%281%29.pdf.

—. 2016. *Formulation, Implementation, Approval and Correction Procedures of Development Projects in Public Sector*. Dhaka: Ministry of Planning.

—. n. d. 'The Fifth Five Year Plan', viewed 10 February 2018 http://www.plancomm.gov.bd/site/files/87d366f2-20ff-4d0f-8ee7-539b44f48f19/-.

Gortner, H. F., K. L. Nichols and C. Ball. 2007. *Organization Theory: A Public and Non-profit Perspective*. Belmont, CA: Wadsworth Thomson Learning.

Grameen Australia. n. d. Viewed 14 April 2018. https://grameen.org.au/.

Grameen Bank, Bangladesh. n. d. Viewed 14 April 2018. https://grameenbank.org/.

Gujja, B. M. Pimbert and M. Shah. 1998. 'Village Voices Challenging Wetland-Management Policies: PRA Experiences from Pakistan and India'. In *Whose Voice? Participatory Research and Policy Change*, edited by J. Holland and J. Blackburn. London: International Technology Publications.

Haider, S. K. U. 2011. 'Genesis and Growth of the NGOs: Issues in Bangladesh Perspective'. *International NGO Journal* 6(11): 240–7. doi: 10.5897/INGOJ11.025.

Hakim, M. A. 1987. 'The Colonial Legacy in the Administrative System of a Post-colonial State: The Case of Bangladesh 1971-1985'. PhD thesis. Carleton University.

Hakim, M. A. and A. S. Huque. 1995. ‘Governmental Change and Constitutional Amendments in Bangladesh’. *South Asian Survey* 2(2): 255–70. doi: 10.1177/097152319500200208.

Haque, M. S. 2002. ‘The Changing Balance of Power between the Government and NGOs in Bangladesh’. *International Political Science Review* 23(4): 411–435.

—. 2004. ‘Governance Based on Partnership with NGOs: Implications for Development and Empowerment in Rural Bangladesh’. *International Review of Administrative Sciences* 70(2): 271–90. doi: 10.1177/0020852304044255.

Harland, C. 1991. Nijera Kori: Bangladesh. In *Projects with People: The Practice of Participation in Rural Development*, edited by P. Oakley et al. Geneva: International Labour Office.

Hashemi, S. M. 1996. ‘NGO Accountability in Bangladesh: Beneficiaries, Donors and the State’. In *Beyond the Magic Bullet: NGO performance and Accountability in the Post-Cold War World*, edited by M. Edwards and D. Hulme. West Hartford, CT: Kumarian Press.

Heeks, R. 2008. ‘ICT4D 2.0: The Next Phase of Applying ICT for International Development’. *Computer* 41(6): 26–33. http://www.nixdell.com/classes/Tech-for-the-underserved/heeks-ictd2.pdf.

Helfer, B. 2006. ‘The Relationship between Technical Assistance and Intended Outcomes in the State Improvement Grants in Special Education’. PhD thesis. The George Washington University. UMI Number 3237038. ProQuest Dissertations and Thesis Database.

Hickey, S. and G. Mohan, eds. 2004. *Participation from Tyranny to Transformation: Exploring New Approaches to Participation in Development.* London: Zed Books.

Holland, J. and J. Blackburn. 1998. *Whose Voice? Participatory Research and Policy Change.* London: IT Publications.

Hossain et al. ‘Participatory Budgeting in Bangladesh Local Government Context’. 3(2): 28–43. https://pdfs.semanticscholar.org/38c2/b2c37bc31bc5726b0f51e9d7c83ec83a1f3c.pdf.

Hoyle, A. 1990. ‘The Role of the Civil Servant in Development’. In *Government and People: Issues in Development*, edited by M. Campbell and A. Hoyle. Canberra: University of Canberra.

Ika, L. A. and J. Donnelly. 2017. ‘Success Conditions for International Development Capacity Building Projects’. *International Journal of Project Management* 35(1): 44–63. doi: 10.1016/j.ijproman.2016.10.005.

Islam, M. S. 2016. 'The NGOs Sector in Bangladesh: Emergence, Contribution and Current Debate'. *Advances in Asian Social Science* 7(2): 1182–88.

Islam, R. and G. Walkerden 2015. 'How Do Links between Households and NGOs Promote Disaster Resilience and Recovery?: A Case Study of Linking Social Networks on the Bangladeshi Coast'. *Natural Hazards* 78: 1707–27. doi: 10.1007/s11069-015-1797-4.

Jahan, F. 2006. 'Public Administration in Bangladesh'. *The State of Governance in Bangladesh 2006*, Working paper 1. Dhaka: Centre for Governance Studies, BRAC University.

Jamil, I. 1998. 'Transactional Friction between NGOs and Public Agencies in Bangladesh: Culture or Dependency?'. *Contemporary South Asia* 7(1): 43–69. doi: 10.1080/09584939808719829.

—. 2002. 'Administrative Culture in Bangladesh: Tensions between Tradition and Modernity'. *International Review of Sociology* 12(1): 93–125. doi: 10.1080/03906700220135363.

Karim, L. 2008. 'Politics of the Poor? NGOs and Grass-Roots Political Mobilizations in Bangladesh'. *Political and Legal Anthropological Review* 24(1): 92–107. doi: 10.1525/pol.2001.24.1.92.

Karim, M. 1996. 'NGOs in Bangladesh: Issues of Legitimacy and Accountability beyond the Magic Bullet'. In *Beyond the Magic Bullet: NGO Performance and Accountability in the Post-Cold War World*, edited by M. Edwards and D. Hulme. West Hartford, CT: Kumarian Press.

Kelegama, S. 2012. *Foreign Aid in South Asia: the emerging scenario*. n. p.: SAGE.

Kenny, S. 2016. 'Community Development Today: Engaging Challenges through Cosmopolitanism?'. *Community Development Journal* 51(1): 23–41. doi: 10.1093/cdj/bsv058.

Kentor, J. and T. Boswell. 2003. 'Foreign Capital Dependence and Development: A New Direction'. *American Sociological Review* 68(2): 301–13.

Kochanek, S. A. 1997. 'Bangladesh in 1996: The 25th Year of Independence'. *Asian Survey* 37(2): 136–42. http://www.jstor.org/stable/2645479.

Kosack, S. and J. Tobin. 2006. 'Funding Self-Sustaining Development: The Role of Aid, FDI and Government in Economic Success'. *International Organization* 60(1): 205–43. http://www.jstor.org/stable/3877872.

Kothari, U. and M. Minogue. 2002. 'Critical Perspectives on Development: An Introduction'. In *Development Theory and Practice: Critical*

Perspectives, edited by U. Kothari and M. Minogue. Basingstoke, Hampshire: Palgrave.

Krull, B. C. 1999. 'Popular Participation in NGO Sustainable Development: Projects in Maya Biosphere Reserve, Peten, Guatemala'. PhD thesis. University of Wisconsin-Madison.

Kumar, S., N. Kumar and S. Vivekadhish. 2016. 'Millennium Development Goals (MDGs) to Sustainable Development Goals (SDGs): Addressing Unfinished Agenda and Strengthening Sustainable Development and Partnership'. *Indian Journal of Community Medicine* 41: 1–4.

Lange, M. K. 2004. British Colonial Legacies and Political Development'. *World Development* 32(6): 905–22. doi: 10.1016/j.worlddev.2003.12.001.

Leal, P. A. 2007. Participation: The Ascendancy of a Buzzword in the Neo-liberal Era'. *Development in Practice* 17(4–5): 539–48. doi: 10.1080/09614520701469518.

Loudon, M. and U. Rivett 2013. Enacting Openness in ICT4D Research. In *Open Development: Networked Innovations in International Development*, edited M. L. Smith and K. M. A. Reilly. Cambridge, MA: The MIT Press.

Lukensmeyer, C. J. and L. H. Torres. 2006. 'Public Deliberation: A Manager's Guide to Citizen Engagement'. *Collaboration Series*. Washington D.C.: IBM Center for the Business of Government.

Lunt T., J. Ellis-Jones, K. Mekonnen, S. Schulz, P. Thorne, E. Schulte-Geldermann and K. Sharma. 2018. 'Participatory Community Analysis: Identifying and Addressing Challenges to Ethiopian Smallholder Livelihoods'. *Development in Practice* 28(2): 208–26.

Lusthaus C., M. H. Adrien and M. Perstinger. 1999. 'Capacity Development: Definitions, Issues and Implications for Planning, Monitoring and Evaluation'. *Universalia Occasional Paper*, no. 35: 1–21.

McAnany, E. (2012). 'Saving the World: A Brief History of Communication for Development and Social Change'. Illinois: University of Illinois Press/ProQuest Ebook Central. https://ebookentral-proquest-com.ezproxy.canberra.edu.au/lib/canberra/detail.action?docID=3414195.

Makuwira, J. J. 2014. *Non-governmental Development Organizations and the Poverty Reduction Agenda*. Oxon: Routledge.

Mallick, R. 2002. 'Implementing and Evaluating Microcredit in Bangladesh'. *Development in Practice* 12(2): 153–63. doi: 10.1080/09614520220127676.

Maniruzzaman, T. 1976. 'Bangladesh in 1975: The Fall of the Mujib Regime and its Aftermath'. *Asian Survey* 16(2): 119–29. doi: 10.2307/2643140.

Mcloughlin, C. 2011. 'Factors Affecting State–Non-governmental Organisation Relations in Service Provision: Key Themes from the Literature'. *Public Administration and Development* 31(4): 240–51. doi: 10.1002/pad.611.

Merino, S. S. and I. de los Ríos Carmenado. 2012. 'Capacity Building in Development Projects'. *Procedia – Social and Behavioral Sciences* 46: 960–67. doi: 10.1016/j.sbspro.2012.05.231.

Miller-Dawkins, M. 2014. *Global Goals and International Agreements: Lessons for the design of the Sustainable Development Goals*, working paper no. 402, Overseas Development Institute.

MLAA (Madaripur Legal Aid Association). n. d. *Training and Capacity Building*, viewed 14 April 2018. http://mlaabd.org/training-capacity-building/.

Mohan, G. and Stokke, K. 2000. 'Participatory Development and Empowerment: The Dangers of Localism'. *Third World Quarterly* 21(2): 247–68.

Mohanty, C. T. 2003. *Feminism without Borders: Decolonizing Theory, Practicing Solidarity*. Durham, NC: Duke University Press.

MoHFW (Ministry of Health and Family Welfare). n. d. *Health, Population and Nutrition Sector Development Program (HPNSDP)*. viewed 22 November 2018. http://www.mohfw.gov.bd/index.php?option=com_content&view=article&id=166&Itemid=150&lang=en.

Moser, C. and Sollis, P. 2006. 'Did the Project Fail? A Community Perspective on a Participatory Primary Health Care Project in Ecuador'. *Development in Practice* 1(1): 19–33. doi: 10.1080/09614524910007602l.

MoWCA (Ministry of Women and Child Affairs). n. d. *Totthoapa Prokolpo*, viewed 6 October 2022. https://totthoapa.gov.bd/.

—. n. d. Totthoapa. 'E-monitoring Template', viewed 6 October 2022, https://totthoapa.gov.bd/wp-content/uploads/.

Moyo, D. 2009. *Dead Aid: Why Aid is Not Working and How There is a Better Way for Africa*. London: Penguin Books.

Nakibinge, S., D. Maher, J. Katende, A. Kamali, H. Grosskurth and J. Seeley. 2009. 'Community Engagement in Health Research: Two Decades of Experience from a Research Project on HIV in Rural Uganda'. *Tropical Medicine & International Health* 14(2): 190–95. doi: 10.1111/j.1365-3156.2008.02207.x.

Nargis, M. n. d. 'Scaling-Up Innovations Community Clinic in Bangladesh'. PowerPoint presentation, viewed 17 August 2019. https://www.who.int/pmnch/about/governance/partnersforum/4a_nargis.pdf.

NGOAB (NGO Affairs Bureau [Bangladesh]). 2013. *Report on The Role of NGOs in Socio-Economic Development in Bangladesh*. Dhaka: NGOAB.

NGOAB (NGO Affairs Bureau [Bangladesh]). n. d. *FD-6 Foreign Funded Project Sample Template*, viewed 19 September 2019. http://ngoab.portal.gov.bd/sites/default/files/files/ngoab.portal.gov.bd/forms/d9baae9f_273a_44f9_af3c_a55a73041859/FORM%20FD-6.pdf.

—. 2022. *List of All NGOs*. Viewed 17 December 2022. http://www.ngoab.gov.bd/site/page/4623023a-745a-4593-8633-96c6cbda7f97/List-of-Local-NGOs

NILG (National Institute of Local Government). n. d. *Training and Consultancy Division*, viewed 14 April 2018. http://www.nilg.gov.bd/site/page/19256d65-b5d7-466c-b3f9-a13ecfe53497/প্রশিক্ষণ-ও-পরামর্শ-বিভাগ-সম্পর্কে.

Oakley et al. 1991. *Projects with People: The Practice of Participation in Rural Development*. Geneva: International Labour Office.

Oakley P. and D. Marsden. 1984. *Approaches to Participation in Rural Development*. Geneva: International Labour Office.

OECD (Organisation for Economic Co-operation and Development). 2015. *Stakeholder Engagement for Inclusive Water Governance*, viewed 22 January 2019. https://www.oecd.org/gov/stakeholder-engagement-for-inclusive-water-governance-9789264231122-en.htm.

—. n. d. *OECD Glossary of Statistical Terms*, viewed 14 February 2019. https://stats.oecd.org/glossary/glossary.pdf.

Paul, S. 1987. *Community Participation in Development Projects: the World Bank experience*. World Bank discussion paper no. 6. World Bank: Washington D. C.

PKSF (Palli Karma-Sahayak Foundation). 2012a. 'Project Preparation Guideline', viewed 13 February 2018. www.pksf-bd.org.

—. 2012b. 'Policy of PKSF for Monitoring & Evaluation', viewed 13 February 2018. www.pksf-bd.org.

—. n. d. 'Partner Organisations', viewed 25 February 2018. http://pksf-bd.org/portal/web/?page_id=185.

PPRC (Power and Participation Research Centre). 2016. *Bangladesh 2016: Politics, Governance and Middle Income Aspirations Realities and Challenges*. Dhaka: PPRC.

Purvis, R. L., T. J. Zagenczyk and G. E. McCray. 2015. 'What's in It for Me? Using Expectancy Theory and Climate to Explain Stakeholder Participation, Its Direction and Intensity'. *International Journal of Project Management* 33: 3–14. doi: 10.1016/j.ijproman.2014.03.003.

Rahman, S. 1990. 'Bangladesh in 1989: Internationalization of Political and Economic Issues'. *Asian Survey* 30(2): 150–57. http://www.jstor.org/stable/2644893.

—. 2006. 'Development, Democracy and the NGO Sector: Theory and Evidence from Bangladesh'. *Journal of Developing Societies* 22(4): 451–73. doi: 10.1177/0169796X06072650.

Raihan, S. 2008. 'Trade Liberalization and Poverty in Bangladesh'. *Macao Regional Knowledge Hub No. Working Papers*, No. 1. https://mpra.ub.uni-muenchen.de/37905/.

—. 2012. 'Policy Priorities and Role of Aid in Least Developed Countries: Bangladesh'. In *Foreign Aid in South Asia: The Emerging Scenario*, edited by S. Kelegama. Delhi: SAGE.

RDRS. n. d. *Training Courses*, viewed 14 April 2018, http://www.rdrsbangla.net/training-center/.

Reality of Aid. n. d. 'The Reality of Aid 2018: An Independent Review of Poverty Reduction and Development Assistance', viewed 24 January 2019, http://www.realityofaid.org/wp-content/uploads/2018/12/Full-Version-RoA-Report-2018-min.pdf.

Riddell, R. C. 2007. *Does Foreign Aid Really Work?* Oxford University Press.

Rist, G. 2007. 'Development as a Buzzword'. *Development in Practice* 17(4–5): 485–91. doi: 10.1080/09614520701469328.

Roberts, N. 2004. 'Public Deliberation in an Age of Direct Citizen Participation'. *American Review of Public Administration* 34(4): 315–53.

Rondinelli, D. A. 1986. 'Administration of Integrated Rural Development Policy: The Politics of Agrarian Reform in Developing Countries'. In *The State and Development in the Third World*, edited by A Kohli. Princeton, NJ: Princeton University Press.

Sansom, K. 2011. 'Complementary Roles? NGO–Government Relations for Community-Based Sanitation in South Asia'. *Public Administration and Development* 31: 282–93. doi: 10.1002/pad.609.

Sanyal, B. 1991. 'Antagonistic Cooperation: A Case Study of Non-governmental Organizations, Government and Donors' Relationships in Income Generating Projects in Bangladesh'. *World Development* 19(10): 1367–79.

Sarker, A. E. 2005. 'New Public Management, Service Provision and Non-governmental Organizations in Bangladesh'. *Public Organization Review: A Global Journal* 5: 249–71.

Schwittay, A. 2016. 'Muhhamad Yunus: a Bangladeshi aid celebrity', In *Celebrity Humanitarianism and North-South Relations: politics, place and power* edited by A. R. Lisa, Oxon: Routledge.

Sen, A. 1999. *Development as Freedom*. Oxford: Oxford University Press.

Shams, K. 1990. 'People-Centred Development in Asia and the Pacific: The Current Status'. In *Government and People: Issues in Development*, edited by M. Campbell and A. Hoyle Canberra: University of Canberra.

Sillitoe, P. 2000. 'Let Them Eat Cake: Indigenous Knowledge, Science and the Poorest of the Poor'. *Anthropology Today* 16(6): 3–7.

Silverman, D. 2004. 'Research and Theory', In C. Seal (ed), *Researching Society and Culture.* London: SAGE Publications Ltd.

Sjöstedt, M. 2013. 'Aid Effectiveness and the Paris Declaration: A Mismatch between Ownership and Results-based Management?' *Public Administration and Development* 33: 143–155. DOI: 0.1002/pad.1645

Smith, M. L., L. Elder and H. Emdon. 2011. 'Open Development: A New Theory for ICT4D'. *Information Technologies & International Development* 7(1): iii–ix.

Smith, T. 1986. 'The Underdevelopment of Development Literature: The Case of Dependency Theory'. In *The State and Development in the Third World*, edited by A. Kohli. Princeton, NJ: Princeton University Press.

Sobhan, R. 1979. 'Politics of Food and Famine in Bangladesh'. *Economic and Political Weekly* 14(48): 1973–80. https://www.jstor.org/stable/4368187.

—. 1998. 'How Bad Governance Impedes Poverty Alleviation in Bangladesh'. *OECD Development Centre Working Papers*, No. 143. Paris: OECD Publishing. https://doi.org/10.1787/466441620275.

Spivak, G. C. 1999. *A Critique of Postcolonial Reason: Toward a History of the Vanishing Present*. Cambridge, MA: Harvard University Press.

Steger, M. B. and R. K. Roy. 2010. *Neoliberalism: A Very Short Introduction*. New York: Oxford University Press.

Stone, L. 1989. 'Cultural Crossroads of Community Participation in Development: A Case from Nepal'. *Human Organization* 48(3): 206–213. https://www.jstor.org/stable/44126429?read-now=1&loggedin=true&seq=1#page_scan_tab_contents.

Tabassum, N. and S. P. Ahmed. 2014. 'Foreign Direct Investment and Economic Growth: evidence from Bangladesh', *International Journal of Economics and Finance*, 6(9): 117 – 135. URL: http://dx.doi.org/10.5539/ijef.v6n9p117

Tarannum, R. 2009. *Development Initiatives by Foreign Funded NGOs in Bangladesh*. Germany: Verlag.

Taylor, H. 2002. 'Insights into Participation from Critical Management and Labour Process Perspectives'. In *Participation: The New Tyranny?*, edited by B. Cooke and U. Kothari. London: Zed Books.

The Daily *Prothom Alo*. 2022. Report on the Village Courts Project. 15 October 2022, 3.

Thomas, P. N. 2014. Development Communication and Social Change in Historical Context. In *The Handbook of Development Communication and Social Change*, edited by K. G. Wilkins, T. Tufte and R. Obregon, 7–19. Wiley Blackwell.

Too, E. G. and P. Weaver. 2014. 'The Management of Project Management: A Conceptual Framework for Project Governance'. *International Journal of Project Management* 32(8): 1382–94. http://dx.doi.org/10.1016/j.ijproman.2013.07.006.

Tosun, C. 2000. 'Limits to Community Participation in the Tourism Development Process in Developing Countries'. *Tourism Management* 21: 613–33.

TIB (Transparency International Bangladesh). 2007. *Problems of Governance in the NGO Sector: The Way Out*, Dhaka: Transparency International Bangladesh.

Turner, J. R. 2004. 'Five Necessary Conditions for Project Success'. *International Journal of Project Management* 22(5): 349–50. doi: 10.1016/j.ijproman.2004.02.001.

UCEP Bangladesh. n. d. 'Our Partners', viewed 30 November 2018, http://www.ucepbd.org/#our-partners.

UN (United Nations). n. d. 'United Nations Millennium Declarations', viewed 19 April 2019, https://www.un.org/millennium/declaration/ares552e.htm

UNDP (United Nations Development Programme). n. d. 'Millennium Development Goals', viewed 19 April 2019. https://www.undp.org/content/undp/en/home/sdgoverview/mdg_goals.html.

UN. 2021. 'Mobilizing Private Sector Investment towards SDG Financing', 13 December. https://bangladesh.un.org/en/169745-mobilizing-private-sector-investment-towards-sdg-financing.

Unwin, T. 2004. 'Beyond Budgetary Support: Pro-poor Development Agendas for Africa'. *Third World Quarterly* 25(8): 1501–23. doi: 10.1080/0143659042000308492.

Uphoff, N. 1992. 'Local Institutions and Participation for Sustainable Development'. *IIED Gatekeeper Series*, No. 31. https://www.researchgate.net/publication/242463814_Local_Institutions_And_Participation_For_Sustainable_Development.

WBG (World Bank Group) 2018. Strategic Framework for Mainstreaming Citizen Engagement in World Bank Group operations: engaging with citizens for improved results, viewed 24 January 2019 https://openknowledge.worldbank.org/handle/10986/21113?locale-attribute=en.

WHO (World Health Organization). n. d. 'WHO to Continue Supporting Community-Based Health Activities in Bangladesh', viewed 17 August 2019. http://www.searo.who.int/bangladesh/COMMUNITY_based/en/.

Willis, K. 2011. *Theories and Practices of Development* (2nd edn). New York: Routledge.

Zafarullah, H. 2007. 'Bureaucratic Elitism in Bangladesh: The Predominance of Generalist Administrators'. *Asian Journal of Political Science* 15(2): 161–73. https://www.tandfonline.com/doi/abs/10.1080/02185370701511339.

Zafarullah, H. M. 1987. 'Public Administration in the First Decade of Bangladesh: Some Observations on Developments and Trends'. *Asian Survey* 27(4): 459–76. https://www.jstor.org/stable/2644683.

Zafarullah, H. M. and A. S. Huque. 2001. 'Public Management for Good Governance: Reforms, Regimes, and Reality in Bangladesh'. *International Journal of Public Administration* 24(12): 1379–1403. doi: 10.1081/PAD-100105944.